My Storm
By
Carolyn A. Ames

To my sister, Donna. I love you Chilibean.

Introduction

We all must weather storms in our lives to some degree. How we handle the storm depends on its intensity, duration and damaging effects. It depends on how much experience we have, the support and encouragement that surrounds us, and our ability to rebuild once the destruction has passed.

Storms are created by a combination of elements coming together at one moment. The elements themselves are benign and go unnoticed until, at a moment in time, they are brought together to form a powerful entity strong enough to rock your foundation, to rock you to the core of your being.

In a moment, the life you lived becomes something you do not recognize as yours any longer. Everything has changed. The storm races in, blowing away all the normalcy of the day, pounding down your plans and washing away relationships that you thought were steadfast. As the floodwaters rise you search for high ground, solid ground that you can trust to save you from immediate danger – a respite that will allow you a few minutes to breathe and to think about how to slow down the churning storm.

My Storm begins with a calmness that lulls you into a security that each day will be better than the day before. Slowly, like a magnet, the elements of life come together, causing friction and electricity. The storm builds and you begin to sense that something serious is about to happen. Then it hits hard, with more velocity than you were prepared to endure. This is **my storm**.

~ Carolyn A. Ames

Chapter 1

Fire and Brimstone

I stood still among the sagebrush, breathing in the musty cologne of the monstrous thunderhead that was quickly crossing the prairie. A low rumbling growl was coming from its belly. The fine hairs of my arm stood up as the winds danced around me in electrifying excitement. It was warm and wild watching the storm approach. My heart hastened with each magnificent boom.

I imagined I was in a Western movie and this was a stand-off between nature and I. It didn't matter that the rattlesnakes hiding among the brush would be my only witnesses or that the oil rigs didn't care one way or another. I was surely the bravest 14 year old girl the thunderhead had ever challenged. Although I was only 100 yards from the dirt alley that led to my house, it felt as though I were far from town, amongst the rim rocks, horny toads and turquoise treasures. Midwest, Wyoming was nothing like Western Washington.

My parents divorced when I was six years old. My Mom had moved my sisters and me from Alaska to Western Washington two years later and remarried a man with two children of his own. It made my stomach ache each time I thought of not seeing my Dad. I missed him so much. Luckily, it was mostly at night when I thought of him, so my tears could flow freely and privately. My sadness gave me a sense of isolation which, in turn, created a deep loneliness.

When I was eleven, Dad invited my 9 year old sister, Donna, and I to stay the summer with him in this new land called Wyoming. He worked as a Deputy Sheriff and reminded me of the Winston Cowboy with his boots, hat, and belt buckle. After a few summers we decided to try living with Dad and his new wife Cindy during the school year and go to Washington in the summer. It was then that I experienced the true nature of a storm.

Playing under Washington's huge towering evergreen trees, luscious ferns and salal made the transition into the wild Wyoming prairie shocking with its enormous sky, crackly rolling sagebrush and grassless terrain. At first I thought the land was flat and empty. I was thrilled to discover that it was full of life, cliffs and ravines. It didn't just rain. The storms raced over the land with nothing to stop them, building up enormous thunderheads like the one now approaching me. Just as you thought it would speed by without even noticing you, it would cast out dust devils to throw dirt in your eyes, hovering just long enough to pelt marble sized hail on your head until you ran for shelter. Then the real show of force would begin. I was shocked to see so many lightning bolts splitting through the dark sky at once but it was a thrill that I looked forward to every time I smelled that musty cologne.

The rain was coming down now in big glops. A warning that nature would win this showdown and that I best be on my way home. I decided that I was no match for this thunderhead, and made my way back around the four oil rigs to the dusty alley that bordered my back yard. Just as I reached the sliding back door hail began to fall. It was going to be another fantastic display of power. I could feel it in my bones.

* * * * *

Sunday

The storm the night before was as wonderful as I had hoped; I felt a sense of spirituality whenever nature showed off. This morning was Sunday morning, however, and time for my soul to get whipped into shape with a weekly dose of old time religion.

I battled with myself to actually get out of bed and not fall back into a dream that I was already getting dressed. My legs tensed and relaxed as I stretched in an effort to get the blood flowing to my brain. It felt great when my toes cracked. I could get out of bed and into the shower with only opening my eyes into little slits, and then pretend I didn't wake up at all and let my mind drift in and out of thought.

After showering I made my bed, which was a new chore for me. Cindy insisted on it or, rather, my dad insisted that she insist on it. Cindy was 9 years younger than my dad and only 11 years older than me so she was eager to solidify her role as the step-mother and wife. Either way, I didn't mind since I had my very own room that was painted my very own colors. Imagine bright, in-your-face orange for walls and then yellow and orange bedding. I couldn't believe my dad let that happen! Then, right in the middle of my bed, I placed the humongous orange shaggy pillow that Cindy had made for me as the cherry on top of my bed sundae. It was a sight to behold!

We attended church on Sundays at the Open Bible Church. It was a Pentecostal church built with fire and brimstone. Donna and I had learned quickly that sleeping during Rev. Dewey's sermons was a big mistake. As soon as one of us would begin to drift off to dream about the mansions made of silver and gold in heaven, Rev. Dewey would jump off the stage and yell "Hallelujah!" Our eyes would bulge wide open and there he would be with his jolly, Santa-like belly still jiggling from the 3 foot vertical jump and a huge satisfied grin brimming with caffeine-stained teeth. Rev. Dewey enjoyed children and had a great sense of humor. His two daughters were very active in the church and we aspired to be as Christian as they were.

It was a very short drive to church. Midwest was only one mile from Edgerton and the church was just inside the boundaries of the little town. Edgerton was bigger than Midwest and had all the bars, a bowling alley, a hotel and a store slightly bigger than the Midwest store. Midwest didn't have much more than the school but that made up the difference since students from both towns went there. We had to drive over a cattle guard that signaled we were in Edgerton. These guards were made of metal pipes that laid across the road about an inch apart creating a short bridge. Cattle supposedly were afraid to cross over the bridge because of the gaps between the pipes. I'm not sure if they were trying to keep cattle in town or out of town since I never did see any there.

Once we entered the church the energy surged as everyone welcomed everyone while wearing their Sunday best smiles and complimenting each other on their Sunday best outfits, trying hard to think of Bible verses they could quote on the fly. The softly worn wooden pews beckoned us to sit down and stay awhile. We always sat on the left side of the church in the second row from the front by the aisle. Donna and I sat through "grown up" church, which was torture. First of all, we were wearing dresses and couldn't put our ankle on our knee like my dad did. We had to do it the "girl" way and cross them over which was not comfortable at all. Donna and I were tom-boys but tried very hard to be as girly as possible on Sunday. We figured this was to teach us patience.

Rev. Dewey signaled everyone to stand so we took the cue and grabbed the old leather bound hymnals from the back of the pew in front of us. This was our favorite part, the singing. Sometimes Rev. Dewey would take requests. Donna and I would raise our hands as straight and high as possible while standing on our toes and screwing up our faces to be taller. Our greatest hope was that he would call on one of us. We knew which songs were fun and which were boring. This was the moment that would define the next two hours. Would we fade into a stupor of slow drawn out songs about walking through a valley to die, or would we march like soldiers in circles around the church singing loudly "Onward Christian soldiers!...marching off to war!...with the cross of Jesus!...going on before!...." Everyone would have to join in, young and old. That would keep us wide awake for the sermon!

Donna and I smiled as hard as we could, trying to send telepathic pleas through God to our pastor. He was, after all, the vessel God used to give us His messages. We were only requesting a small message come from us while He was at it. Rev. Dewey was thoughtful for a moment as he scanned the sinners up and down the aisles. He started to point way in the back to Mr. Rogers. Donna and I squirmed. No! Not Mr. Rogers! He will pick a song we don't even know or understand! Just when our hopes were dashed Donna saw the end of Rev. Dewey's finger aligned with her gaze. He picked Donna! Hooray! It was her turn to choose the first song, so she paused dramatically, as if torn between a ballad and a sonnet. I glanced at the church members and could see the older folks rolling their eyes. They knew what they were in for and that they would have to march. Donna didn't disappoint them! It was going to be a wonderful day of faith!

Once the singing and marching was over everyone settled into prayer with flush cheeks and sore feet. The sermon began and I slowly dazed out. I looked like I was paying attention and that was the secret. I could pick out key Holy words coming from Rev. Dewey's blessed mouth and create the most beautiful, peaceful place that I imagined would be my little slice of heaven.

Just as I found my happy place I was jolted back to my wooden pew. Donna's eyes were like saucers and then I saw why. Rev. Dewey was bounding across the stage in a theatrical performance. His voice bellowed as he dared Satan to tempt him. His face was becoming a glowing bright red and I started to fear he would have a heart attack.

He went on for a while and then as a grand finale he drew back his right leg and kicked Satan as hard as he could. Now this would have been very soldier like except that Rev. Dewey underestimated his kick ability. His right leg went forward as high as his head and down Rev. Dewey went with a thunderous echo right on his hind end. There was pure silence as the faithful tried to decide what the best reaction would be. Donna and I held our breath and laughter the best we could with little giggles escaping from the corners of our mouths. However, there was no reason to be concerned. Rev. Dewey was a professional. He had gone to college to become a reverend. He probably studied about this exact type of situation. Rev. Dewey laughed and laughed...at himself. When he finally caught his breath and rose back up to the pulpit he smiled a glorious smile and said, "Well, I think God is telling me to be a little more humble!" With this statement I knew for a fact that Rev. Dewey was truly a man of God.

* * * * *

Sunday afternoons were a time to relax, read the newspaper and eat fresh ham sandwiches. After church my stomach would scream for food. Surely, I would wither and die at any moment if I didn't get to make that ham sandwich. Our ham was fresh and not pre-cut from a deli. I would cut it a quarter inch thick and introduce it to my homemade bread, mayo, mustard, cheddar cheese and dill pickle slices for crunch. Normally, my taste buds would rebel against mustard but with ham it was pure chemistry.

We lived an hour's drive from a real grocery store so we bought meat by the side (side of beef, side of pork) and shot our own venison. Once, dad decided we should raise and butcher our own chickens. It was so disgusting, we never did it again. My sister and I were traumatized by headless chicken bodies running around in circles. The smell of boiling chicken feathers, in an effort to remove them, was like rotting Easter eggs or the sulfur creek that ran outside of town

After the chicken experience dad decided we would raise a pig, which Donna and I promptly named, not realizing that we had just domesticated that pig in our minds. Seeing our new pet turned into ham, chops, bacon and lard was a difficult lesson for us to learn. Ham does not taste the same when it has a name. Luckily, the ham on my sandwich came from an unnamed pig that I had never met. It was as heavenly for my tongue as the Sunday sermon was for my soul.

I carried my sandwich and large glass of milk around the kitchen to the dining area where Donna was already seated with the colored comics section of the paper. Without a word, she passed the middle page of the three pages over to me. We worked well together when it came to things we both enjoyed. Fighting was rare for us now and never physical like when we were younger. Back then hitting each other was easier to deal with and got the fight over quickly. Once we matured we switched to the "silent treatment" and it was difficult. How long should the treatment last? Should it include the evil eye or mean faces? Maybe both?

As I savored my ham sandwich, alternating between it and the milk, I thought about the last time I had used the silent treatment on Donna. I had been in my room when the arguing escalated and I had warned her not to take a single step into my room. She was at my bedroom door considering my threat and I restated it in a harsh evil tone to let her know I was not playing around. What she did next shocked me to the point of paralysis. She did not step foot into my room-not an inch. Instead she spit into my room. Yes, spit, with all the saliva she could muster, flew out of her mouth with an arch like a grenade and splattered out amongst my orange shag carpet. Donna was shocked at what she had actually done. Then, slowly, her expression changed to fear. Everything was in slow motion for a moment before I leaped from my bed. Donna ran like an Olympic Sprinter to her room upstairs. I couldn't catch her before she slammed her door shut and leaned against it. All that was left for me to do was the silent treatment. It lasted for hours. I hated it. Eventually, I was so exhausted from not talking to her that I gave up. It didn't take very long for us to make up when we fought. Nothing was ever quite as important as having each other to talk to.

"Switch." Donna said it simply and matter-of-factly. It was part of the comic page system we had developed. She was done and ready for the middle page. We swapped without even looking at each other. Once I finished my ham sandwich, rinsed out my glass and placed my dishes in the dishwasher I went to my room to lie down for a while. Sunday afternoons were lazy. I could take a nap, write a letter or listen to music.

Just as I started to doze off my phone rang.
"Hello?" I managed to mumble in my half sleep.
"Whatcha doin'?" It was Donna calling me from her room upstairs.
We had discovered by accident that we could call each other's phone (we had the same number) if we dialed really fast and hung up, then picked up again like we were answering.
"I'm taking a nap, why?" I rolled over on top of my shaggy pillow.
"I'm sooooooo bored. Wanna go outside?" Donna asked in her deep humming voice.
When she was little it took a couple years for her to grow hair and everyone thought she was my little brother. I loved her voice, especially when she would sing. That voice meant I could do no wrong. I always felt confident and in charge around Donna. Not in a bullying way but in a responsible way; I was a leader and Donna let me be the leader because she loved me.
"Okay, let's go but I'm going to be Miss Saturn", I insisted. There was a pause as she pondered what planet she would be.
"I'm Pluto then," she finally decided.

Once outside in the dry heat of summer we crossed the grassless yard toward the only object in it. It was an old rusty metal swing set with no swings, just the frame. Each end of the frame had a bar across it in an "A" shape and that was all we needed to get our imaginations going. Donna stood on one bar and I was on the other bar. We imagined we were on the stage and instead of Miss America we were contestants in the Miss Universe pageant. I was Miss Saturn surrounded in beautiful rings of gold and crimson and Donna was...well... Miss Pluto. We sang "It's a Small World After All" over and over then danced sexy for our audience of crab grass and ants. Then finally the moment would come to pick a winner but the judges couldn't decide between us. We would end in a tie every time.

We didn't have to help with meals on Sunday so when Cindy called us in to dinner we raced to get washed up. Cindy was a gourmet cook and we would devour everything on the table if manners didn't get in the way all the time. Donna worked hard on keeping her left arm on her lap instead of surrounding her plate with both arms as if she were guarding it from starving wolves. I struggled to cut my meat without having my elbow up in the air. Once dinner was done, leftovers put away and dishes washed, we went to church for the evening worship. For a day of rest, Sundays were pretty exhausting.

* * * * *

Monday

It was that lazy summertime period right before school was to begin. Most of our friends were still on vacation or with their parents school shopping. We had plans to go school shopping on Friday and since all the clothing stores were an hour's drive away, Cindy planned to take us in to work with her during the morning. Then we would have lunch before spending the rest of the afternoon shopping.

This was our second year of school clothes shopping with Cindy and we were prepared. The year before (our first time) we were in a daze. It was hard for Donna and me to wrap our minds around the fact that we were going to have all brand new things. When we lived with our mom, we wore a lot of hand-me-downs and would get some new clothes for Christmas. This was a different type of shopping, with new pants, new shirts, new underwear, new bras, new jackets and belts as well as new shoes and boots. We quickly discovered that we could choose anything we wanted as long as it was a "Western" style which immediately felt confining since it required you to tuck in a long sleeve plaid shirt into your corduroys and then buckle your belt. I wondered how long it would take to undo everything when I had to pee.

Another issue was the fact that we had to wear socks and boots most of the time when we were used to going bare foot. By the time I was fully clothed it felt like I was a knight clad in armor. Sweat covered my brow and I was faint with starvation. Shopping for new clothes was a test of endurance, and I was receiving a failing grade.

I was sure the second year would be different. I knew what to expect and could prepare. I had hinted about how stylish I thought cowl neck sweaters were, they would match almost any color of corduroy pant so they were practical and warm. Secretly, I prayed that plaid was out of style and not available in stores. I would find out on Friday.

It was only Monday. Cindy had left us our chore list which was only two pages long since we had just cleaned everything on Saturday. Most of the Monday list had to do with preparing for dinner so Donna and I divided it up so our time could be spent doing anything else besides chores. It was my turn to dust the living room so I grabbed the feather duster and walked to the bookshelves. We had a police base radio on one of the shelves and a red phone that was off limits. If it rang, it was dispatch and meant an emergency. Dad had a set territory to protect which encompassed many miles of travel in his 4x4 Bronco police vehicle. His job was exciting to us. Donna and I used to stare at the red phone and imagine Dad answering it, then throwing on his cape to fly to the rescue. We figured it must be similar to the phone the President of the United States had in his house and maybe it was a direct line to the President, we couldn't know for sure.

"What are we gonna do today?" Donna wondered out loud as she swept dirt into a dustpan. We were alone until 6pm during the weekdays unless Dad stopped by.
"I dunno, what do ya wanna do?" I managed to ask while dusting the oil lamp.
"Wanna go to the pool?" Donna asked.
"No, it's closed remember?" I answered.
"Wanna go to the school?" Donna asked and then quickly laughed one big "HA!" before saying, "I rhymed!...wanna go to the pool...wanna go to the school!"
I rolled my eyes. Donna had gotten into the habit of only laughing one syllable...HA! And that was it, no more than that. It was funny to see other people's reactions when she would do it; how they expected more and didn't get even one more HA!

We decided to walk to the school and then to the store. Besides the post office and a joke for a park, those were the only destinations you could actually name as a place to walk. By walking first to the school and then the store, we would, by default, automatically walk past the post office and the park. On the way back we could take a path that would go right past the Mondle's house to see if any of the four boys were around. It was a great plan.

The temperature had really heated up when we finally left the house. It would be another scorcher. The roads had only been paved a year ago. It was surprising to see them buckle and melt under the dry heat. We stepped off the concrete sidewalk onto the soft gooey pavement with our bare feet. We carried our shoes in case Dad showed up unexpectedly. It was so hot we ran toward the closest shade. I put the sole of my right foot up against my left calf and then alternated back and forth until they cooled down enough to make it to the next shady spot. We could have put our shoes on and walked with no problem on the road surface but it wasn't fun to do it that way. We only had a few hours before the mercury would rise to 112 degrees and we needed to be back home by then.

After a few blocks of stop and go running and comments about frying eggs on the pavement we made it to the school. Midwest High School was a K-12 school. It was the first school I had ever seen that went from Kindergarten to 12th grade. One hall housed K-6th grade, another hall supported 7th-8th grade classes. A separate building contained classes for 9th-12th grade, a cafeteria and the administration offices. The gymnasium, pool and locker rooms were connected to the administration office area by a commons area. Donna and I walked around the school grounds looking for friends. The school was still locked up and the play areas were still abandoned. No luck this time.

As we started to walk toward the store we scanned the area one last time and were delighted to find an old lot full of crusty flat cow pies. Sometimes cattle trotted through town since Midwest didn't have cattle guards to stop them. They would come in from the prairie at night and make their way through the alleys and streets. As a result, cow pies could be found on old lots where the cattle congregated. I picked up one of the dried up pies and threw it like a Frisbee. Donna laughed and quickly did the same. Before we knew it, cow pies were flying everywhere. We started throwing them at each other. The pies would crumble as they hit our bodies. I ran to a corner of the lot where I had spotted a large pie. My heart was full of joy when I realized it was still soft in the center!

Donna pummeled me with another scabby pie as I retaliated. I didn't mean to hit her in the face but in my excitement I underestimated the strength of my throw. Her face had a look of horror when the pie careened off her cheek leaving behind a warm green goo of poo. I rushed to apologize but it was too late. She had found a juicy one for me and evened the score.

Once we were sufficiently amused and felt that the day wasn't completely wasted, we headed west toward the store. The homes were all very similar as we walked the blocks. They had all been built at the same time when the oil wells were drilled. Square houses with square yards on square blocks all in neat rows. We made a right and then a left toward the post office. There were no mailboxes so everyone had to get their mail from the post office. During the summer we walked to the post office every day. We were greeted at the door with a cool wisp of air that rushed past us and into the heat of the day. It died a quick painless death.

"We got mail!" Donna yelled in excitement as she twisted the key and pulled open the little metal door. It was a letter from Mom. Since the envelope was thick we figured there were letters from our baby sister, Tara and from our step-sister, Terry as well. We wouldn't open the letter until we were home. It needed the proper attention and gave us something to look forward to.

After Donna locked the mailbox back up and put the key in her front shorts pocket we made our way to the store, bought Pepsi and Twinkies to replenish our energy, and turned for home. If we had continued on the road past the store we would have ended up in a tiny housing area called "Gas Plant". I never did understand why it had a name since there were only small old houses there with dirt roads…nothing else. I had a feeling that it wasn't a great place to live but had nothing to back that up. Across the street from the convenience store was the city park. It was about the size of our yard but with some grass and a fence on the back side to protect people from accidentally falling down the dirt cliff. We couldn't understand why anyone would think of it as a park. There were no swings, no barbeque pit and no picnic table. We never saw anyone at the park and figured that even the bull snakes would be bored there.

"Eeewwwwwahh…" Donna crinkled up her nose in disgust.
"It's Salt Crick", I said in response to the putrid smell in the air.
"I know it is. It's like farts." Donna breathed in deep to be sure that it really did stink like a fart.
She had gone swimming in Salt Creek with a friend last summer and Dad had gotten mad. He said it was dangerous. There was quicksand and we could get stuck. I envisioned the creek filled with toxins and bubbling like a poisonous soup. A

poisonous fart soup that would make you smell bad forever no matter how much perfumed talc powder you wore.

"Come on, we need to get home" I coaxed.

"What about the Mondle boys?" Donna begged. She loved boys and if you could see four boys at one place and time, well that was like winning a lottery.

"Tomorrow, it's too hot now and we have our letter to read" I reminded her.

"Oh yeah! The letter! Let's go! Why are you so slow!" she yelled as she skipped away toward home.

* * * * *

Our house was on a corner lot at the northern most part of town. It was nice that we were on the last road and only had the oil field behind us. The house was originally one of the small old white houses you could see up and down the streets but once Dad was done with it, it was the largest house in Midwest and it was barn red. We ran in the door and grabbed some fresh iced tea before sitting down to read our letter. Donna opened it very carefully in case something might fall out. There was one letter to both of us from Mom, two letters from Tara written in crayon, and two letters from Terry. We smiled knowing we had hit the jackpot.

I started with my letter from Tara. There was a heart with a happy face on the front. It was folded like a card. She had worked hard on the heart shape. Under the red crayon she wrote "To: Sissy" in blue crayon. I loved that she called me Sissy. I missed her so much. I opened the letter and inside she wrote, "I miss you Sissy! I love you verry much!" It was written in blue as well. Under the words were flowers, all smiling. Then at the very bottom she wrote "From: Tara". On the back she drew another heart that was smiling. Tara had just turned 7 years old and was the sweetest thing on God's great Earth. Take sugar, honey and corn syrup, mix it up and it wouldn't be as sweet as my baby sister. I was 7 years old when she was born and made it my business to help take care of her in any way I could. Donna and I loved her from the moment we saw her.

Next I read the letter from Terry. Terry was my step-sister and 5 months older than me. I matured faster than she did so everyone thought I was older. It didn't really matter to either of us though. Terry was left-handed so I knew her writing right away. She had that left-handed slant. She used pencil and wrote really small so that I had to squint to read her letter. She had a crush on a boy. Mom took her to get her school supplies and they bought her two new shirts – one was a cowl neck sweater! How lucky!

Once Donna and I were done with Tara and Terry's letters I opened the letter from Mom and read it out loud. She told us all about Tara's birthday dinner which was always tacos. She let us know how Tigger, our little female cat was doing and how the weather was. Then she told us how much she loved us and missed us. By the time I was done reading the letter Donna had gotten really quiet. We missed Mom a lot and wished we could just open an invisible door, walk through it, and we'd be in our home in Washington giving her a big hug. We were just there for the summer and the transition from one home to the other was difficult.

"Well", I finally said as I folded up the letter, "we better get started on dinner".
Donna grunted and rolled around on the living room carpet.
"I'm not making the salad" she said with her nose and mouth in the carpet so that she sounded like she was in another room.
"I'll make it but you'll owe me", I offered.
"Kay." Donna always said okay when I told her she owed me. I figured that someday I'd figure out what she should owe me but for that moment it just sounded good.
She drug her legs up under herself and stood for a split second and then, dramatically, fell back to the carpet in a spread eagle form as if she was exhausted from doing absolutely nothing and teased, "Well, you better go make that salad!"
I crossed my eyes at her then reminded her that she still had to help set the table. She rolled back over on her face, mumbled something about the universe being unfair then got up and headed toward the silverware drawer.

After dinner and dishes Cindy reminded us to shower. Donna and I smelled extra...well...cow pie-ish but Cindy would have fainted if she knew about that! Dad had gone up to watch the news so Donna headed to the bathroom upstairs and I headed to the bathroom in my room. Once I got into bed I waited for a few minutes and then rolled over, picked up the phone and dialed my number quickly then hung up. It was fun to talk to Donna from our rooms, especially since Dad and Cindy had no idea we could do it. It gave me an internal giggle, like a stomach giggle that didn't quite make it to the vocal chords. I picked the phone back up and heard my sister's voice on the other line. We had never been separated and weren't about to let having our own rooms do it now.

* * * * *

Tuesday-Thursday

The next three days were pretty much more of the same except on Wednesday night when we were back at church again for Bible Study. Cindy had decided that we were mature enough to handle Bible Study and we liked it because it often involved potlucks. You could always count on some type of jell-o dessert and Mrs. Dill's potato salad. It was nothing like my mom's potato salad but it was the closest we would get. Everyone always ooh'd and ahhh'd at Cindy's dishes. She would pull out a gourmet recipe from a secret recipe book that required secret ingredients we couldn't even pronounce. We imagined that was so that we couldn't tell anyone.

On this particular Wednesday there was a change of events. We walked into the church annex to find the furniture set up like a game show with six chairs on each side of the podium. In front of each set of chairs was a narrow table with a big button on the table in front of each chair. Rev. Dewey had a huge smile on his face and was rubbing his hands together in excitement. Once everyone was seated he explained that the church youth groups throughout Wyoming and neighboring states were participating in a contest. Every two weeks we had to learn specific chapters in the Bible and then six participants from each group would compete with another church to answer questions and quote verses. The furniture was set up to show us how it would look.

I didn't really hear the rest because my mind took off on its own. A competition! I loved to compete! Donna and I were the first to sign up. We had to wait until Sunday Youth Group to find out what chapter to study but it didn't take long for us to figure out that Wednesdays would be used to practice as well. We thought that was fantastic!

* * * * *

Friday-Saturday

"Carolyn, get up" Cindy called from my bedroom door, "It's shopping day!" I looked over at my alarm clock. 5:30am! No way! I had been used to getting up around 9:00am so this was very painful to my internal clock. We had to ride into town with Cindy and hang out at her work until noon which meant we had to look presentable for her boss. No shorts, no flip flops and our shirts had to be tucked in. Usually when we rode into town it was for the monthly grocery shopping. We had fun grocery shopping. First of all, it meant food which we loved. Secondly, we each got to push a cart and finally, it made Cindy really happy which often led to the rare trip through a DQ drive through for ice-cream.

The hour drive to town was timed by natural markers such as "Teapot Rock" at Teapot Ranch. The prairie land was deceptively flat until the highway took a quick right twist around a ravine and then slithered up a hill and saddled up to the ranch. All of a sudden you could see the homestead, the horses and the rim rock above it shaped like...you guessed it...a teapot! I wondered who lived there and why. Donna wondered if there were any kids, and if they went to school. We could always expect to see herds of antelope no matter what time of the day it was. It was hard to tell the difference between antelope and deer when we first came to this land but now it was simple. The pronghorn antelope reminded me of a deer and goat mixed together. They weren't shy and sometimes the entire herd would be on the highway.

About 30 minutes into the journey we could see Casper Mountain in the distance. I thought it was funny that it was called a mountain since I had been raised around mountains in Alaska and Washington and this one was more like the foothills of Mount Rainier rather than an actual mountain. I could understand why it would be considered a mountain though since there was nothing on the prairie that was quite so high. Casper Mountain created a cruel illusion of being close to our destination since town lay at the foot of the mountain, grasping at its shin with new homes and mini ranchettes. There was a winding string of trees going through town that marked the river.

Once we entered the city of Casper it only took minutes to drive anywhere and before we knew it, we had arrived at the law office. Donna and I knew the drill and were quiet, sweetly behaved young women with only smiles for Cindy's boss and co-workers. They had no idea that we were wondering how long our suffering would be and if anyone would notice if we had to pick our underwear out of the crack of our butt. We tossed and turned on the hard chairs while looking at Sports Illustrated and Home and Garden magazines. They didn't have Archie comics or teen magazines so we assumed it was rare that a teenager needed to sue anyone.

At exactly noon we left for lunch, and then to go shopping – no DQ this time. Suddenly we realized that instead of heading to the clothing stores we were pulling into a fabric store. Cindy was very excited and announced that this year she would be sewing our clothes. Everything except our pants anyway. I was alarmed and wondered if she actually knew how to make a cowl neck sweater. I needn't have worried however, because she had picked up on my hints. After we left the fabric store we headed to the mall and I chose a warm rust colored cowl neck sweater and a matching pair of corduroys. I desperately wanted Levi jeans but knew better than to ask. If I had Levi's, I would wear them every day of the week.

Saturday was cleaning day. We hated Saturday. Our Washington Saturdays were filled with sleeping in, playing outside, eating, visiting relatives, and laying out in the road looking at the stars of heaven. Needless to say, Saturdays were different with Cindy. She was raising us to be *refined*. Throughout the week we did the basics such as dishes, vacuuming, dusting, prepping for dinner and our rooms. On Saturday it was taken to a higher level of cleaning. We not only repeated the weekly chores but we also wiped down everything including the baseboards, scrubbed the bathrooms, washed the laundry and ironed all of our clothes. Then we would have a project chore such as cleaning out the pantry or refrigerator.

Ironing was a chore that took some practice and when Donna melted her rayon shirt we learned two things; rayon shouldn't be ironed and melted rayon is very difficult to remove from an iron. We ironed pillow cases and folded them in thirds, being careful to iron after each fold. We even had to iron our pants. Usually we saved ironing until the evening so it could be done in the utility room while Cindy was sewing. This way it felt more like Little House on the Prairie instead of prison.

Sometimes Cindy would bake all day on a Saturday. That was pure torture because we couldn't sample or sneak anything. There were fresh homemade doughnuts, turnovers, cinnamon rolls, zucchini bread, banana bread, five kinds of cookies, cakes, pies and more. Dad hovered over the doughnuts which was rather ironic since he was a police officer. He was a master at sneaking, and we could only hope to one day learn from the master. It was even harder for us since Cindy put us on a diet with her. I'm pretty sure this was Dad's idea, because she seemed a little anxious about it. We started eating more chicken breast and Melba toast dinners. Each morning we would weigh ourselves and write it down in one column on a yellow legal pad. In the next column we would write down how many pounds we had lost or gained. At the end of each week Dad would pay us a dollar per pound lost (see why I'm pretty sure it was his idea?).

Once the weigh-in started we lost a pound per day - at least on paper. The truth was that the first week we really did shed a few pounds but we didn't care. Donna and I had no desire to lose weight but we did enjoy money. Money was a rare commodity back in Washington. There were seven of us in one house with only one person working outside the home. Leroy, my step-father, worked every single day but it was barely enough to pay the mortgage. We had food but Mom had to be careful when grocery shopping. We ate a lot of hamburger, hotdogs, and cornflakes, and money wasn't something that could be handed out for an allowance, let alone a lost pound of fat. Food was never wasted at my Mom's house and we all ate quickly to get to the seconds. Choosing to eat chicken breasts and Melba toast was as strange to us as ironing pillow cases.

Donna and I learned quickly how to work the system. We weighed ourselves and marked down that we lost a pound then we would walk to the store and use our money to buy food. The first thing Donna bought was Twinkies. She bought two packs of two Twinkies and ate all four Twinkies before we were two blocks from the store. I told her that she was taking it a little too far, but the only response she gave me was a very satisfied grin. I couldn't blame her. I would buy a Pepsi and a candy bar. Eventually, Cindy stopped the weigh-ins. I wondered if Dad had been paying her per pound as well.

After chores, I tried to spend a few minutes outside to smell the earth. The dirt, the air and the sage told me secrets of the coming night. My skin responded to the slightest caress of the wind. Breathing deeply through my nose and raising my chest, I would fill my lungs with the knowledge that I am a part of all of it. I am nature.

Chapter 2

Law and Disorder

School started earlier in the Midwestern states. Instead of waiting until after Labor Day, the first day was usually during the third week of August. The year before, we were new to the school. It wasn't difficult to fit in at all though, because anything or anyone new was immediately popular. I had never experienced instant fame or the silliness that goes along with it. By the end of the first two weeks I had said yes to 'going steady' with a boy, and then had broken up with him without even ever talking to him. Girls were running back and forth setting relationships up and then breaking them back down. I just sat at the cafeteria table and watched in awe as my very own soap opera was being played out. Luckily for me I wasn't the only naïve 8th grader, so nothing more was expected and the game soon ended.

Donna and I were excited for school to start because that meant our friends would be back in town. Donna had a lot of friends - mostly boys - and a couple really close girl friends. She was very sociable. I tended to have one or two friends total at a time and enjoyed time by myself to draw or write. A lot of times Donna would have a friend over after school and they would run amuck throughout the house. She'd pay me to do her chores so she could focus on being a "good host". I didn't mind since I liked her friends and I was entertained by the crazy ideas they came up with.

Dad had taken the week off so we could have one last hoorah before school started. His idea of a hoorah was to look for rocks. Dad was many things; deputy sheriff, church elder, youth group leader, emergency medical technician, teacher, etc... but he especially loved playing his guitar, shooting photos and being a rock hound. Donna and I just loved spending time with Dad, whatever he might be doing. He was especially excited to show us a new place out in the Wild West that was glittering with agates, turquoise, and jade. If we were lucky, we may even find old creek beds crammed with nuggets of gold. Dad was a dreamer and when he dreamed, he dreamed big. He told us that was the *only* way to dream, so we did it too.

It didn't seem like we had driven very far before taking a dusty barren road to the left that headed out toward a crusty set of rim rocks. We went down a ravine and back up a hill before coming to an abrupt halt. The road hadn't ended. There was an entire herd of sheep in the middle of the road complete with lambs running to the safety of their mothers. It was a wonderful surprise. Apparently, they were not familiar with cars and showed no interest in moving so my Dad had to get out of the car and flail his hands in the air, yelling at them to move on. It was turning out to be a very entertaining day indeedy!

When Dad jumped back in the car he was breathing hard and saying something about those "dadgum stupid wool sweaters". Donna and I quickly turned toward the other window as if we had been so intensely scanning the earth for riches that we really didn't hear him. In actuality, we were trying our very hardest to think of anything else besides how funny it was that Dad was flailing at sheep.

"We're here!" Dad exclaimed as if we were supposed to be able to tell the difference between this special ravine and the fifty un-special ravines we had just driven through. We piled out of the car and started following the ravine. It was still muddy on the bottom which was surprising for this time of year. Dad reminded us to watch for rattlers as we scoured the cliff walls from left to right.

Dad bought us our first pair of boots and taught us how to take care of them. Mine were white and tan with a steel toe. Carefully, I would apply the wax to my boot and rub it into the leather. We did this together-my dad, my sister and I. It wasn't until this very moment that I realized cowboy boots were for protection against the rattlesnakes, and not just a fashion statement.

I looked at my cowboy boots and imagined a rattler flying through the air, hooking its salivating fangs into my thigh just above the knee. I would scream in pure agony, Donna would cry in horror and Dad would calmly pull out his 13 inch hunting knife slicing open my jean in one swing without touching my skin. He would then hand the knife to me, directing me to twist it into the bite wound and then to suck out the poisonous blood and spit it into the ravine. In the meantime, Donna would rip the sleeve off her plaid shirt and wrap it tourniquet style around my upper leg. We would then finish our rock hunt.   Until that happened, however, I was content to look for agates.

We started up hill. My feet kept sliding backward so I grabbed at loose sage that gave away. Finally, I got on my hands and knees trying to avoid the cockleburs. I secretly wished I could be barefoot; it would make this much easier. I looked between my hands to see microscopic red spiders scattering. What could they possibly eat?
"Come on girls!" My Dad was already to the top and moving away.
Donna was in front of me so I pushed her on the butt to help her up the steep hill. The air was dry so we didn't sweat but my lips were chapped and we had dust in our eyes.

Once we were at the top it was surprising to look back and see how far we had actually climbed. We ran after Dad only to discover he was already down in the next ravine. He had his camera and told us to walk out onto the ledge. I looked to the right. The plateau we were on went out to a point creating a ledge over the ravine. The cliff of this ledge was over 100 feet above the bottom of the ravine.
Donna said, "No way, Jose!"
I was considering the risk. Dad yelled up again, waving his camera. He wouldn't put me in danger, would he? If the ledge gave way or I fell could he put all my pieces back together again? I knew he could splint any broken bones and apply pressure to any bleeding but what if I broke my back? Would he pray to God and a miracle would happen? Finally, I decided that a miracle would happen if he prayed so I slowly inched my way out onto the ledge.

Donna yelled to me, telling me not to go, which made me want to prove my courage to her even more. Once I made it out to the ledge I looked down at my father. He had a look of surprise that seemed mixed a little with horror. Didn't he think I would do what he asked? He yelled up again and told me to sit down. After he took the picture, Donna and I followed the path he had taken down. I turned and looked up at the ledge then gasped in horror at how precariously the ledge jetted out from the cliff. There was a crack at the base and I knew then that the ledge could have given way at any time. I turned to look into my father's face so I could know if it was a test or just a foolish dare but he was already yards away searching for rocks. Donna stood by me. She thought I was brave but I knew I had been foolish.

We had made a full loop back to the car. I had a handful of agates in my pocket but no silver, gold or jade. The only turquoise I found was so small that one of the red spiders could have carried it home. Donna loved agates and dreamed of finding opal someday. We were tired and ready to go home. The dusty road looked like a lazy rattler's back as the setting sun tipped the rim rocks in melting gold. Donna was sound asleep as I wondered if Dad would brag about his foolish daughter that sat on the edge of death. He had the picture to prove it.

* * * * *

"Girls, come out back, I want to show you something," Dad called to us the next morning.

I looked at the clock. It was 7am! Geez, what is wrong with these adults? They sure don't know how to appreciate sleeping in very well. I pulled on my jeans from the day before, threw on my bra and a t-shirt, grabbed my boots and headed for the sliding glass doors that led to the back yard. Donna wasn't there yet. I ran up to her room to get her. When I opened the door she was laying on the bed with no covers and her butt up in the air. Her knees were tucked under her, arms straight to her sides and her face was to the side with her mouth gaping open. I realized right away that she hadn't even come close to stirring when Dad yelled to her. He didn't have a loud yell and Donna was a deep sleeper.

"Donna, get up! Dad wants us outside now." I shook her while I spoke.

As she came to life I put on my cowboy boots. They were pretty scuffed up from the rock hunting, cliff climbing and death-defying I had done the day before.

"Why is he waking us up so early?" Donna asked after looking at the time. The right side of her face was red from laying on it with a diagonal crease going from the bottom of her cheek to her forehead. The crease had little designs that matched her pillow case.

"I don't know," I answered, "but we better get down there."

Dad was way in the back by the alley. We went out to the back porch which was just a slab of concrete and walked down the dirt driveway to where it met with the alley. Dad had parked his police Bronco there and unloaded three large round rocks, setting them gingerly on the ground. Donna and I looked at each other out of the corner of our eyes. We were woken up early to look at rocks?

"Come here girls," Dad said softy as if he might wake up the rocks if he were too loud.

Lord forbid if the rocks didn't get to sleep in on their vacation!

Once we squatted next to the rocks we realized they looked like dinosaur eggs. They were egg shaped and about a foot tall.

"What are they, dad?" Donna asked as she lost her balance and promptly fell backwards. Talking and squatting at the same time in the morning proved to be too challenging for Donna. I didn't laugh at her because Dad was coming back with a hammer and screwdriver. Instead I looked at her like she was an immature baby. She wasted no time in up-righting herself and sticking her tongue out at me; being sure to squint her eyes dramatically to prove it was out as far as she could get it to go.

Dad started chipping at the first dinosaur egg. I wondered if the baby dinosaur was still alive! Maybe it was a dragon with wings. What if we discovered something no man had ever seen? We would be on the cover of National Geographic and 4th graders everywhere would do research papers on us. Dad didn't talk as he worked which made me hold my breath. I asked him if I could try and he handed me the hammer. He instructed me to be very careful because if I hit the egg too hard it could shatter and that was very bad. The rock was very hard and I could barely crack it.

"Let me do it!" Donna demanded. I made the ugliest face I could at her and then focused again on the goal. I tried two more times before Dad told me to give Donna a try. Donna smiled, grabbed the hammer and proceeded to whack Dad in the forehead with the hammer as she was coming up to swing down.

"Damn it Donna!" Dad yelled (much louder than in the morning), "watch what you are doing! Give me that." Dad grabbed the hammer back from Donna as tears welled in her eyes.

I frowned too and I wanted to hug her. Dad had never sworn at either of us and it was a shock to hear it. Dad had a good way of making us feel really stupid. I think it was because we tried our best to be perfect girls for him so the impact of his words struck us with more force.

Dad made a few more attempts at cracking the eggs and then told us to go play. He would call us once he was able to get them open. We weren't having fun anymore so we quickly moved toward the house.

All of a sudden Donna yelled back to me, "There's a mouse!"

Sure enough, a little field mouse was right up by the back door. He didn't move as Donna approached him. I yelled back to Dad that we had a mouse and it looked tame. Dad yelled at us to leave it alone. The temptation to pet Mickey Mouse was too strong for Donna so she put her finger on its back to stroke the fur. The mouse put its tiny hands around Donna's finger and bit down so hard it drew blood. Donna screamed and flung her hand in the air trying to shake it off. The mouse held true and would not let go.

I envisioned the mouse eating Donna's finger, then her hand, her arm and so on. I didn't know what to do so I screamed too. Finally, Dad ran over and beat the mouse into submission. He squeezed the bite so any germ-laden blood dripped onto the ground.

He was fuming mad as he chastised her, "What are you? Stupid? I told you not to mess with the mouse. Get inside and get a Band Aid."

Once he took a look at Donna's sad, scared face he relaxed and told her it would be okay.

The goose egg on Dad's forehead was turning green. It would heal. The damage done to Donna's heart would scar and stay forever. It was the first twinge of disappointment I had ever felt toward my father.

When Dad finally cracked open one of the rocks we discovered that it wasn't a true dinosaur egg. It was filled with shiny white and purple crystals. We thought that was cool but sleeping in would have been better. Apparently, he sensed that as well because he took them away. They were just too dangerous around Donna and me.

* * * * *

The next day Dad let us sleep in. He had a meeting with his Cadets that lasted the first half of the day. I wanted to be a Cadet really bad, but you had to be 16 years old to join. They wore police uniforms and performed duties at the fairs, rodeos and other community functions. My Dad had started up the Cadet program in an effort to give the teens something to do besides party and get into trouble. They couldn't wear guns but my Dad taught them how to repel down cliffs, save lives, prepare for riots and plan for disasters. Previously timid teens would become leaders to their peers and you could see the pride when they wore their uniforms.

My Dad had been promoted to Sergeant and was recognized for his hard work. Cindy proudly applied his stripes to the sleeves of his perfectly pressed uniforms. In Wyoming, citizens enjoyed the Right to Bear Arms and it took someone with a lot of gumption to have a career in the police force. There was one city cop in Midwest and one state trooper that lived down the block from us but their jurisdictions were very limited. The state trooper kept to the highways while my father's jurisdiction covered every inch of the county.

When Donna and I spent the first summer with Dad he had come into our bedroom the first night and instructed me to roll over as close to Donna as possible. He lifted the mattress and pulled out an M-16 he had stashed there. It was in case of a riot. We were an hour away from any real "backup" so he had to be prepared for everything.

There were weapons hidden all over the house of which we had been unaware. Of course, the hunting rifles were in plain sight just like any other house. It wasn't until we came home one Sunday evening from visiting Cindy's grandma that I found out about the hidden armory. That night it had been dark in the house, without any lights on and Donna was the first to walk in after Dad turned the key. She took two quick steps before realizing she had stepped on something that obviously shouldn't be on the floor. Dad ordered her not to move and switched on the light as we stood in the entry way. Our house was destroyed. Pieces of glass, papers and desk accessories were at our feet. Dad's desk had been ravaged with the drawers left open. We stood frozen in the doorway as Dad un-strapped the pistol from his chest harness. He commanded us with a motion of his hand to stay still and quiet. There was no problem there – I don't think we could have moved if we had wanted to.

Dad made it slowly to the dispatch radio, called for backup, and then called my Grandpa. Grandpa lived in Edgerton and took part in just about every job available. He drove the ambulance, worked with Dad as a volunteer Deputy and with the Cadet program. Donna and I knew him best as Grandpa, a sweet loving man that put family before everything else.

Once Dad gave the all clear we gingerly tiptoed around all our belongings. Drawers had been tipped over throughout the house, the gun cabinet was shattered and empty, and the couch cushions were scattered. Dad had raced up stairs and confirmed that the knives, grenades and M-16s were gone. So were the smoke bombs and riot gear. This meant two things to me; Dad had a lot of weapons we didn't know about and whoever robbed us did know about them. It was clear that the weapons were the first to go, and then the belongings. It had to be someone that knew us or at least knew we were out of town. Cindy cried out as she rounded the kitchen. The path to the backdoor went through the kitchen and the laundry/sewing room. I looked at the floor and saw a line of belongings that had been left behind. The door was still open so we had scared them off when we drove up. Cindy's sewing machine was next to the entrance. One more minute and her most prized possession would have been gone.

As the investigation began, Dad went with the other officers out the back. This was during the winter and snow was still on the ground. The tire tracks were still visible from the back door to the alley and beyond, but the snow was falling again and they had to work fast if the tracks were to be of any help.

I went to my room with mixed emotions. I was anxious to see what was left, hoping that the robbery was directed only toward my parents...hoping that the robbers would think my things were too childish and girly to steal or that they would have an ounce of mercy when they noticed it was a young girl's room. It was hard to direct my anger when I discovered that I wasn't spared. How do you direct your anger and fear toward an unknown? Even in church the unknown has a name, description and story to go with it. Why would anyone want to steal my few belongings?

My silver necklace with a "C" pendant was gone. The music box my Dad had given me years ago when I missed him so much was gone. They had used my robe and pillowcases to carry out everything that was on my dresser. I didn't have anything that was worth a lot of money but I had plenty of treasures with sentimental value that couldn't be replaced.

I laid on my pillowcase-less bed in shock. Someone had gone through my private things, had handled them without caring who gave them to me or why. It felt as though they had handled me with dirty hands. Their plan didn't include thinking about how upset the "girls" would be or whether Cindy's sewing machine had made quilts for the church bazaar. They didn't care that Dad was prepared to protect and serve in the face of disaster or that he had saved lives both from death and from sin. It didn't matter to them that the music box my Dad had given me years ago helped me to deal with the pain of missing him. Who could be so heartless?

Donna and I went home with Grandpa that night and stayed with him through the week while Dad and Cindy took inventory and worked to get the house back in order. Sleeping in my room was never the same after that. It took several nights to feel good about sleeping again. I reverted back to sleeping with my old stuffed animal, Eeyore, throughout the night. I always wondered if I knew the robbers or stood by them in the grocery store line. I would never know. The robbers were never found and our belongings were never recovered. These unknown criminals took away my sense of security forever that evening. Even with all the weapons a person could realistically possess, there is always a vulnerability that cannot be protected.

* * * * *

It was after 1:00pm when Dad came home from the Cadet meeting. He announced that they were planning a huge disaster drill for the county. It was the first of its kind in the State of Wyoming. He was in charge of setting everything up; from the story plot to the make-up, beginning to end. This was his passion.

Dad made special effects such as skin wax, fake blood, blisters for burns and broken bone particles. He practiced on me once by giving me a broken leg with a bone (made with a chicken bone) sticking out of my jeans. He poured blood on it and it was very realistic. I hobbled over to my friend's house across the street and when her mother opened the door I asked for a band aid. She and my friend started screaming and ran for the phone to call for help. I had to stop them right away and show that it was a fake. My Dad was that good.

All afternoon and the next day we talked about Dad's plan. Everyone was to be a part of the disaster; from the hospital emergency room, county and city police department, ambulances, schools and fire department. The plan was to respond to a large-scale realistic disaster and measure whether the county was prepared for such a thing. It would be set up about 10 miles outside of Casper for the sake of timing.

The plot was simple; an oil tanker loses its brakes and t-bones a school bus full of high school students then catches on fire. Donna and I volunteered to be burn victims after considering the different injuries and acting roles involved. Donna and I would be his guinea pigs as well. We were excellent patients and knew how to act, whether we were diabetic burn victims or mangled with broken bones and in shock. We knew if we should just lay listless and moan or scream in agony.

Practically the entire school was going to be involved. Dad had set up meetings already to go over the logistics and direct different groups on how to behave and act. Not only was this good for the different agencies involved but it was also very beneficial for the community to have so many young people · participating in such an important challenge. I considered this role as more important than being a Cadet and vowed to give it all I had. Donna wanted to be sure she could lay by her friends so they could "suffer" together and if they were lucky they could lie next to some really cute boys. I rolled my eyes. So much for being realistic!

* * * * *

For our last day off with Dad, we went to the annual policeman's barbeque. We headed into Casper and then turned left on the old highway toward the park on the eastside of town. Donna and I were shocked by the number of cars! We had no idea there were so many "coppers" in the county.

We were allowed to run free while Dad told war stories with his fellow officers. No doubt one of the stories would be about the hatchet man that ran though town a few years ago.

The *Law* (my Dad, two city cops and the state trooper) spent all night trying to capture the hatchet man. Dad had instructed us to turn on all of the lights in the house and to wait up until he came by to say everything was okay. We were petrified! Why should we have the lights on? Wouldn't the hatchet man be able to see us better with them on? Apparently, Dad did not realize we were experts at hide and seek. This was during the time before he had met Cindy so we were alone in the house and not comfortable at all with having all the lights on.

The hatchet man was a big brawly drunk, balding and bearded that had somehow ended up in our little town. He was crazy on LSD and only wearing underwear as he ran through the streets with his hatchet, threatening anyone that got in his way. He didn't seem to have a purpose other than to be crazy. Information circulated quickly that there was blood on the hatchet but since a victim hadn't been found it wasn't clear if this was true or just a rumor. They couldn't take any chances. Strange things happened in these parts from time to time and the hatchet man could not be taken for granted.

We assured ourselves that we could take on the hatchet man. If he came through the door we would pounce on him with the element of surprise and hold him until the police showed up. We would be hailed as heroes and Dad would make us his deputies regardless of our ages.

They never did catch the hatchet man. Dad said he had taken off out of town but he stayed with us as the villain of many dreams. It was a story to be told during every annual barbeque from that day forward.

We were famished after running around the park. There weren't very many kids and the adults were happily drinking. After wondering out loud if police officers got in trouble for drinking and driving, Donna and I stopped by the grill to see what was cooking. The steaks were huge! The man doing the barbequing was huge too. He asked us if we had hearty appetites and we promptly replied that we did. He went on to tell us that the steaks were buffalo steaks and the best of the best.

The steaks were as big as the 8 inch paper plates he gave us. We hauled them over to the nearest picnic table and grabbed the steaks with our hands. We weren't trying to be barbaric, but there weren't any utensils. It didn't matter anyway. The buffalo might as well have been still walking around. It was so tough that my teeth wouldn't even bite into the meat. It was ironic to be so hungry with such a huge steak on my plate. Once our jaws were exhausted we licked all the salt off the steak and went back for corn on the cob.

The police officers were always nice to Donna and me. It was like an extended family. We were safe and cared for. The hatchet man wouldn't have stood a chance.

* * * * *

Dad was feeling fine and smiling a lot when we headed home that night. He didn't have the worry lines in his face or the serious focus in his eyes that told me he was deep in thought and could, at anytime, discover the purpose of life. Tonight was different and we knew it would be like the "old days". We encouraged him all the way home to sing the old songs and tell stories about all his adventures in Alaska. By the time we arrived at the house he was primed and ready for his old guitar. I ran and grabbed it from the closet upstairs; running as fast as I could out of fear that the moment might pass. Back down the stairs I went, rounding the corner to the living room, past the river-rock fire place and to the sliding glass doors that led to the back patio. Dad and Donna were already sitting on chunks of wood…well, Dad was anyway. Donna was struggling with her chunk and kept falling backward.

Once that trusty old musical friend was in his hands, the world became a place of peace and love. Cindy stopped what she had been doing and joined us. It was an unspoken understanding that we all shared - this was the very core of my father, the true essence of who he really was, as if the guitar brought his soul to the surface of his skin. We sat in a circle singing songs from the 70's by *Peter, Paul & Mary*, *Bread* and *Kris Kristopherson* as well as every *John Denver* song we could think of. My father was the Pied Piper of his time.

Drifting off to sleep, I thought of how things had changed just since Dad had married Cindy. I knew that we wouldn't spend as much time with him, that we had to share him with her. I was okay with that and wanted him to be happy. It seemed that instead of the time being shared between Donna, Cindy and I that Cindy was actually added to our side of the scale and something else was weighing Dad down on the other side. Something unknown to me, but something nonetheless, and I had a feeling that it wasn't good.

Chapter 3

Dust Devil

The weekend before the start of my freshman year at Midwest High School finally arrived. Donna was starting middle school as a 7th grader so we both shared the anxiety and expectation of the coming Monday. Our clothes were all picked out, hair cut, nails trimmed and school supplies packed in our bags. Our permission slips for Volleyball were signed and copies of our physicals were attached. Donna's best friend, Mandy, was back in town and Donna had insisted on seeing her the very second she arrived. Mandy was a very small girl with long dark wavy hair. She had beautiful light brown skin from her Hispanic heritage and seemed to always be smiling. I wished for a relationship like they had but I wasn't jealous. I was never jealous of Donna's happiness.

The closest friend I had was Christy. She was one year older than me and seemed older than her age. I had met her in Youth Group over a year earlier but we didn't really talk until I started school. She approached me in the hall and said I should let her know if I needed anything or had any questions.

Christy was really skinny and had frizzy hair like an afro, which seemed to clash with her pale white skin. Her eyes were wide, which made her appear nervous, but her smile was genuine and I appreciated knowing someone in a grade higher than me. I accepted her friendship and it slowly grew into something we both benefited from. It didn't take long to realize we were opposites and people wondered how we could be friends. Christy was troubled at home, at school and with boys so I was happy to see her attending the Youth Group. I thought I could help her, or at least support her in her efforts to walk the straight and narrow.

Both Christy and Mandy planned to attend Youth Group on Sunday and sign up for the Quiz Show. We were supposed to find out what chapter to memorize and then on Wednesday we would practice being quizzed.

* * * * *

Sunday morning began like every Sunday morning and our family took their place in the second pew on the left as usual. As Reverend Dewey began his sermon I made my *I'm listening intently* face and zoned out. I started thinking about the first day of school and how I would wear my cowl neck sweater even if it was ninety degrees. Just as I imagined that everyone, even the upper classmen, would be envious of my new sweater, I was brought back to the present when I heard the Rev say the "F" word. He was quoting I Corinthians, and the parishioners were listening more intently than normal. What was he saying?

"The great book says," Rev. Dewey quoted with sweat beading on his brow, "'Flee fornication. Every sin that a man doeth is without the body; but he that committeth fornication sinneth against his own body.' Chapter 6, verse 18. Fornication, my dear friends, is of the devil...Satan himself! Do not give into temptations of the flesh!"

I looked at Donna to see if she had heard what I had heard but she had her *I'm not listening and I know you can tell* face. And what was that "F" word? Fornication? Whatever that meant, I knew it was important by the way the congregation was "Amen"ing after every syllable. I listened closely to see if I could get more clues as to the meaning of the word, and quickly turned the pages of my new Bible to I Corinthians, Chapter 7. Rev. Dewey was on the 2nd verse, "...to avoid fornication, let every man have his own wife, and let every woman have her own husband." I quickly read ahead to verse 4, something about a woman not having power of her own body but the husband and vice versa with the husband not having any power.

At that point I figured I was out of context and Rev. Dewey had already moved on to teenage pregnancy and adultery. I would have to look it up in the dictionary for a complete definition but I was pretty sure now that it had something to do with giving away all your power once you were married.

As soon as we got home I quietly went upstairs and pulled the dictionary from the bookshelf. I could feel the guilt rising into my cheeks, hot and red. I wasn't doing anything wrong but I knew instinctively that fornication had something to do with sex. I stayed right next to the bookshelf and thumbed to the "F" words. I found it.

for·ni·ca·tion Pronunciation: \,for-nə-'kā-shən\ Function: *noun*

Date: 14th century

: consensual sexual intercourse between two persons not married to each other

The moment I read the definition Cindy walked up the stairs and asked me if I had swept the patio. I stuttered, "I'm going to do that right now", and quickly closed the book. My heart was beating in my ears as I placed the dictionary back on the shelf and ran down the stairs. The Bible, it turned out, was much more than children's stories and would require much more of my attention in the future.

* * * * *

Our patio was tiny and only took minutes to sweep but it had to be done often because of the dirt and the wind. The heat of the summer had baked all the moisture out of the ground, causing it to crack. Little black ants used the cracks for highways, carrying building material and food on their backs in swift execution. A five foot tall dust devil caught my eye as it made its way down the alley, across the main street and into the neighbor's yard. Dust devils were a funny joke to me. They looked just like mini tornadoes, demanding respect, yet they were completely harmless.

I turned my attention back to the ants. One ant was carrying a twig that was three times its size. I was amazed at the sheer strength of the ant and was wondering if a human could lift three times their body weight when all of a sudden I was completely devoured by the dust devil. Dust devils were notorious for changing directions and this one had done just that. It filled my eyes, ears and nostrils with dirt as I held my breath. Apparently the joke was on me.

Once it moved away I took a couple clean breaths of air and watched it dissipate into nothingness. I spit dirt from my mouth and cleared my eyes with my index finger. I looked back toward the ant, blinking quickly to return moisture to my eyes. It had moved about eight inches down the ant highway, completely unharmed by the dust devil. Not only was the highway a clear route but it was also a protection against wind. Those ants were smart! Now I knew why Donna had such affection for them.

When we were young my Dad was stationed in Florida for a short time. While we were there Donna had sat in a nest of fire ants, which are the nastiest most aggressive ants around. They crawled all over her as she screamed. Dad grabbed her and raced her to the tub trying to get the ants off as they attacked his arms. It was very traumatic and I didn't think Donna would ever look at an ant again without screaming.

However, here in the backyard there was a variety of ants that were very small and all black. These ants didn't bite and Donna liked them. A couple of summers back she started naming them and creating stories about them. It was an all-out ant soap opera with plenty of plot and characters. My mom used to always watch All My Children at noon so we had a good grasp of the requirements for a good soap opera. She even had a love triangle going on between three of the ants.

I made fun of her because she wouldn't stop playing with them and, instead of joining the game, I walked over and stepped on several of the ants. Donna came unglued and yelled at me, "You killed Prego!" Tears were coming to her eyes. I felt my stomach start to ache and said how sorry I was and that I didn't think Prego was dead, that she had made it into the ant hole in time. I leaned down and quickly wiped away the dead ant body parts from the impact site and we peered at the ant hole, waiting for even the slightest sign of life. Finally, a black ant came out of the hole and we cheered. Prego was still alive!...or at least her character was. I was pretty sure Prego was on the bottom of my shoe and that we were now looking at the stand-in for Prego but I wasn't about to reveal that to Donna. I decided to redeem myself and listen to the stories about Prego and her son as well as the lives of the neighboring ants. I had to admit, it was a lot of fun watching the ants and before long I found myself adding to the stories as well. The adventures of Prego and her fellow ants entertained us for a full week that summer.

I swept the patio a second time, thanks to the dust devil incident, and went inside to shower. I chuckled to myself as I thought of how I was going to remove the dust "devil" from my skin before going to the church for Youth Group study. Sometimes I really cracked myself up!

* * * * *

Youth Group started with the introduction of our new guests. There were two others besides Mandy and Christy. Although Christy had been to Youth Group in the past we still considered her new because she hadn't been attending for over two months. She looked a little sheepish when Dad introduced her. Mandy had a shy smile when her name was called but Donna made up for the shyness by immediately embracing her in a bear hug. Luckily, Mandy was a flexible girl and able to withstand the pressure of her rib cage collapsing in on itself. Donna couldn't contain the happiness she was feeling and it made us all smile.

Dad was leading the Youth Group now and announced that he would be coordinating the competition. The "Quiz Show" was actually a competition between churches that tested our knowledge and ability to recite Bible verses. The competition was between Pentecostal churches and reached to the National level. We knew that this meant hours of driving in one direction because towns were sparse, but it was a fact of life that we were all used to. The idea of meeting new people was always exciting and well worth the hard work of memorizing scripture in Old English.

We received our assignment; St Matthew, Chapter 6. The entire chapter had to be understood for answering the questions and verses 5 through 15 needed to be memorized by all of us for recital. We had two weeks to study before our first competition so we began by taking turns reading through the chapter. Luckily for us the verses included the Lord's Prayer. It was important to understand the context of the entire chapter and also be able to recite verses so the hour was spent discussing the meaning and we were sent home to start memorizing the verses.

As soon as we left the church my mind shifted immediately to the coming morning and my first day as a high-schooler. There was no way I could start my assignment so I promised myself to get serious about it after school. I didn't know what Donna's plan was since all she could talk about the rest of the evening was how cute Mandy's brother was, how Mandy had met a cute boy during vacation and kissed him in the pool, and how she wondered if there would be any new cute boys at school.

Chapter 4

Electricity

The first week as a freshman was very different than any other because of one thing – Seniors. The seniors took "freshman initiation week" seriously and weren't about to lay down on the job. As freshmen, we knew that if we didn't obey the seniors we would pay dearly for the rest of the year. We were told how to dress, we carried books, we walked down the halls backwards and gave up our desserts. Luckily, our seniors were lenient and didn't bully us too much.

On Friday we followed the tradition of carrying buckets of whitewash, which were a much diluted mixture of white paint and water, up a steep hillside to repair and paint the "M" near the top that represented not only the school but our town. It was renewed every year by the will, sweat and determination of the freshman class. The walk to the hill just west of town seemed to take forever because it was high noon and the heat was intense.

Once we arrived at the hill I took a look at the narrow path lined with rocks that made its way to the all important 13th letter of the alphabet. It was steep with very little to hold onto except an occasional scrawny sagebrush. I had completely underestimated the task but that didn't matter. It had to be done and our class would do it better than any other class. I felt pride in my heart because I knew my class was a force to be reckoned with. We were following in the footsteps of freshmen from years back and so we lined up and grabbed the back of each other's pants and started slowly on our ascent. Our seniors respected our traditional right by throwing tomatoes at us all the way up the path, as was their duty.

Once I made it to the "M" I turned to look down on the town. We were higher than the water tower. The roads were straight and the houses all in neat rows like a checker board. The oak trees looked like little broccoli stems and I wondered how a tall Washington Evergreen would look next to one. I could see my house on the last street with Dad's Bronco parked in the front. My friend, Christy, was walking toward my house. She should have known where I would be so I figured she must be asking Dad to help her practice for the Youth Group Quiz Show. I had forgotten all about it with all the excitement of the week but knew that I could cram for it Saturday night.

My class met back at the school at 5pm on Friday. We received all the details for our freshman float, the parade plans, bonfire and carnival. It amazed me that such a tiny town would have such big plans. But I learned early on that these towns lived and breathed for football, volleyball, wrestling, basketball and homecoming. Even families that could barely make ends meet supported the school. Midwest High School had a state-of-the-art Olympic size indoor swimming pool, gymnasium and track along with high quality PE equipment. Any student that wanted to sign up for a sport was able to play, anyone that wanted to be a cheerleader could be one and if you didn't want to do any of the above you could be in the Band or part of the Booster Club. I had already started volleyball practice and decided to be part of the freshman float team. To my surprise it was okay with Dad and Cindy so after dinner I walked to the shop where the float would be brought to life, with my help.

The night was perfect! The air was cooling from the day and felt exhilarating on my face. It was the first time I had been allowed to leave the house on my own so I walked slowly and soaked in the moment. I could see my classmates being dropped off at the big metal shop just ahead. Although it had only been two and a half months since I had seen them, I felt like a stranger sneaking up on the town. I wasn't originally from this place and there was always a sense of being an outsider, someone that was missing out on a secret.

Vernon made it to the door just in front of me and held it open. He was taller and broader than he had been in the spring. He had a look of confidence in his eyes and smiled easily when he recognized me. We knew each other well and he had written me during the summer in Washington. During the 8th grade we spent a lot of time together and I treasured his friendship. We were always trying to "go steady" which amounted to kissing for us, but it seemed to take away the easiness of our friendship and I would break up with him. Back and forth it would go. Standing with him at the door I thought that maybe we could try again. Everything felt new.

As I entered the shop a large structure took all my attention. It was made of wood and chicken wire. I couldn't make out the shape yet. Lisa directed me toward the colored tissues and quickly showed me how to twist it and attach it to the wire. She did this with each newcomer until all 18 freshmen were accounted for-not a single classmate was missing. Everyone was hard at work with smiles on their faces. This had never happened before and the entire room was energized with the bond we felt.

Skip made his way over to me with more tissue. As he sat next to me I could feel my blood pressure rise and my breathing increase. This was a very new and exciting feeling that needed to be investigated. When I looked over at him I blushed when I saw that he was looking directly at me! He looked right into my eyes and smiled. I smiled and quickly turned away but my heart was ready to beat out of my chest. He was staring at me!

I focused really hard on my tissue as my mind raced. What should I do? He had a wrestler's body, all muscle and defined under his tank top. He enjoyed flexing his muscles in a playful way. His hair was a bleached blond color that contrasted with his tanned skin. As he reached beside me to take more tissue from the pile his arm brushed against my knee. I could feel his strength and smell his Old Spice Sport cologne (my favorite). I glanced at him again and he smiled.
"You have gorgeous eyes," he said.
I thanked him in a whisper. It was all I could get to come out. My pulse was in my neck now and I felt as if I were on a drug. I attached my tissue and an older man walked over.
"Is this fella givin' you a hard time young lady?" he asked.
"Aww Pop!" Skip complained as his Dad took my hand.
"Is my son trying to offer you some of his toe jam?" he asked with a twinkle in his eye.

Skip's face turned bright red as I laughed. Skip and his father spoke about the logistics of the coming events. I was relieved for the distraction since I hadn't realized I had been holding my breath and took the time to inhale a few times.

As I looked around at the progress of our float I noticed Vernon across the room. He had seen the exchange between Skip and I, it was all over his face. He gave me a pain-staking smile and acted like he was fine but I knew him too well. We had no commitment so there shouldn't have been any guilt...but yet there it was. Vernon was the oldest boy of the Mondle boys. Donna had a crush on his brother, Jay. The Mondle boys were fun in every way. They had great imaginations, smiled all the time and were always ready for whatever grand ideas Donna and I would come up with.

Vernon was the only friend that wrote to me while I was in Washington for the summer. He didn't just write a few lines but would tell me all about what he and his best friend Brian were doing every day. We both worried about Brian since his dad was really mean to him. It didn't help that Brian's dad was a city cop either. There were unspoken immoralities in the small town and a father beating his son was one of them. Our quarterback had the same problem so it wasn't even a matter of rich versus poor or strong versus weak. I always wondered if the boys that were hit by their fathers knew that they weren't the only ones.

Vernon started to walk toward me. I didn't realize I had been staring at him while I was thinking about everything. His brown straight hair had the "first day of school hair cut" look. Just as he approached Skip turned back toward me and Vernon stopped.
"What do you want Mondle?" Skip asked.
"N-n-nothing," Vernon stammered, "just saying hi to Carolyn".

It was clear that Vernon felt uncomfortable around Skip for more reasons than I could know. I started to feel uncomfortable for him too and I think Vernon realized that because he quickly said hi and turned away. I wanted to go with him but when Skip put his hand on mine I could feel the warm in my veins go straight up my arm. A rush of energy went through my body as I turned my head. He was looking at my lips and then moved to my eyes.

"Will I see you at the bonfire tomorrow night?" he whispered.
I nodded yes rather than attempt to speak again. He cradled my chin for a moment with his left hand, lifting it slightly and then

glided his right hand over my left cheek to the back of my ear. I could feel tingles in my back racing their way to my neck. I gasped slightly in surprise as he leaned in and kissed me ever so lightly on the lips.

"Good, I'll be looking for you," he said as he got up to leave.

Of course, I just sat there with my lips still numb and my eyes glazed over. He smiled at the lack of response and waved goodbye. I felt so many different emotions that night, new emotions that I needed to feel again. I'd have to wait though. It was time to go home.

Unlike my gradual walk to the shop early in the evening, I ran all the way home. I had to get home before the feelings wore off and before Donna was in bed. I had to tell her all about everything. As I ran, my mind went over the details so that I wouldn't forget a thing... but I had already forgotten about Vernon.

* * * * *

Saturday crawled by, tick by barely moving tock. Every cell in my body was being tortured by the miniscule movement of time. I put extra effort into my chores, trying to focus on scrubbing the toilet with vigor as if cleanliness was going to spin the Earth a little faster. When it was finally 4pm I changed into my cut-off jeans, making sure the little strings were hanging down, and put on a clean tank top. The jeans were short and made my legs seem extra long. I was tan from a summer of basting and had natural blonde highlights in my brown hair. I liked the look and smiled at myself before heading down to the carnival.

The carnival was held down at the football field. It was complete with game booths, barbeques with food and a dunk tank. One of the football coaches was sitting in the dunk tank and all the football players were lined up with their cash. The cheerleaders were standing in a small circle glancing over at the football players and a few boys were staring at the cheerleaders. Amy ran over to me with excitement all over her face. Amy was Christy's younger sister and the oldest of triplets. Even though she was a triplet, she didn't look like the other two. Her other sisters, Brenda and Cathy, were identical until you got to know them. Amy had wild red hair that was wavy and unmanageable. Brenda and Cathy had fine blonde hair that couldn't hold a curl. Once Amy made it to within hearing distance she spoke.

"Skip is here and asking about you! Are you going together? Have you seen him? He's looking fine!" she panted.

I looked around and spotted him in the dunk tank line. Amy and I started to walk over toward the line when the Assistant Football Coach yelled as he splashed down into the tank. A chorus of "Hooray!" came from the line as Boyd, a senior, bowed before his adoring fans.

"That was pure luck!" Amy taunted.

"Oh ya?" yelled another Senior, "Why don't you get up there then and give us something else to look at, like your wet T-shirt?"

That did it. Everyone in line was waving their dollars and yelling for Amy and me to sit in the dunk tank. Amy's face turned beet red but instead of turning and walking away she grabbed my hand and led me to the tank. For the next half hour we took turns in the dunk tank yelling and daring the boys to hit the target. The first time we were dunked the crowd went wild. The water was cold and felt good in the dry, hot afternoon. Dad and Cindy would not have approved of this which made it that much more fun!

It was my turn to get up in the seat again when Amy turned to me and said we had to leave right away. She sounded urgent so I walked a couple of yards away from the dunk tank with her, wondering what the problem was. We were having so much fun.

"What is it?" I asked as she continued to escort me away from the carnival.

"We have to go to your house right now, look down," she said as she pointed to my leg.

I looked down and streams of bloody water were running down my legs. At first I didn't realize what had happened. Did I get hurt on a nail in the dunk tank and not notice it? Then it dawned on me that I had started my period. The water from the dunk tank made it so that I didn't feel anything and my cramps hadn't started yet.

I looked up at Amy in horror at the thought of anyone seeing what had happened. Amy knew exactly what I was thinking.

"No one saw. I pulled you away too fast. Let's go get cleaned up so we can get you back down there!" she said quickly.

I smiled at Amy. She was the free spirit type and wanted to see me hook up with Skip. Amy was already sexually active and I didn't want to tell her that I wasn't even close to hooking up with anyone. French kissing was extreme enough for me at this point.

After I changed Amy and I headed back out but not before Cindy stopped to inform me that I had to be in the house at 9pm. I had voiced my disappointment and received an additional 15 minutes for walking time. The bonfire would barely get going by then and I would miss all the real fun. I was careful not to complain though, some time was better than none and my cramps were fast approaching. Amy assured me that she would give me all the details of anything I missed.

The football coaches lit the bonfire and cheers went up from the crowd. The Head Coach talked about the coming season, expectations and hard work. The cheerleaders performed a couple routines and the booster club talked about membership. As the bonfire grew taller I saw the enormity of it. I hadn't realized before how tall the bonfire was built. Flames leaped 20 feet in the air, swirling around tall boards and pallets. It hypnotized you and beckoned for you to come closer. I was entranced by the pure beauty of it. The 30 foot circle around the fire was lined with students, teachers and parents. It wasn't dark yet but everyone was drawn to the fire as the sun died down and the air cooled quickly on the prairie.

I felt a presence behind me, blocking the cold from my back. It drew closer and as I started to turn around strong solid arms wrapped around my waist. My hands immediately grasped the arms as Skip's voice was in my ear.
"I've missed you."
My hands relaxed and I held his arms to me.
"Good," I teased as I slowly turned around, "because you are going to have to miss me some more. I have to go home in 15 minutes."
Just as he started to protest I saw my Dad talking to one of the cadets over by the bleachers. What was he doing here?!

Not ready for my Dad to see me talking to any boy I walked Skip to the other side of the bonfire. We talked about football and then he showed me how he could jiggle his eyeballs. The feelings from the evening before weren't there. Maybe it was because my Dad was there or because I had issues with eyeballs. I told Skip I wasn't feeling well (which was true due to my cramps) but that I couldn't wait to see him in school Monday. I had a feeling there would be plenty of time to explore my feelings and I was enjoying the newness of them.

I started heading for home and Vernon ran up beside me.
"Heading home already?" he asked.
"Ya, I have to be home early," I confessed.
"Well, I'll walk you then," he decided and proceeded to talk to me about the new Billy Joel song that just came out.

It was as if the awkward moment the night before had never happened and he was still my friend. He walked me as far as the corner across from my house and said bye. I thanked him and crossed the street to my yard. None of the boys ever walked Donna and me up to the door because they were afraid of my Dad. Dad didn't do anything to scare them but just the fact that he was a cop and I was a cop's daughter made it difficult for any boy to take the chance of the door opening and having Officer Dad standing there. I was okay with it though because I was a little afraid of that happening too.

* * * * *

"'*And when thou prayest, thou shalt not be as the hypocrites are: for they love to pray standing in the synagogues and in the corners of the streets, that they may be seen of men. Verily I say unto you, They have their reward.*' The book of Matthew, Chapter 6, verse 5." I nailed it!

"That is correct," Rev. Dewey responded with way more enthusiasm than I expected. He seemed surprised that we had all studied enough to recite our verses. I held my breath as he turned to Christy for her turn.
"Please recite the next verse, Christy," he instructed.

There was no more mister nice pastor. We had to do our best and treat this as if we were competing. I was now thankful for going home early from the bonfire. I studied for two hours before bed and it made a huge difference. I turned to listen to Christy. Apparently, she had been practicing with my Dad so I was surprised that she was so nervous.

She began, "Ummm...'*when thou prayest*'...no wait... '**But thou**, *when thou prayest, enter into thy closet, and when thou hast shut thy door, pray to thy Father which is in secret: and thy Father which seeth in secret shall reward thee openly.*' The book of Matthew, Chapter 6, verse 6." She did it! We all cheered.

I loved those verses. There were people in our church that only came to church to receive a sort of status. As if to say "look at me, I'm so religious and righteous". They never volunteered for the church bazaar or stayed after the service to meet anyone. I always hoped that the Holy Spirit would touch them and bring their soul to the surface of their skin like it did so many others in our church.

We had a large number of adults that spoke in tongues and once in awhile a lucky member of our little congregation would be filled with the Spirit and speak out loud to us. I would get goose bumps on my arms and my hair would tingle. I figured my soul must be speaking with God when that happened. It felt really good and I would lose touch with my body, almost like I was in a dream. It was at times like that when I knew without a doubt that God existed.

Once everyone was done reciting verses we moved on to the questions.

"What," asked Rev. Dewey, "are we asking forgiveness for in verse 12?"

Donna raised her hand to heaven, standing on her tippy toes with her face scrunched up in an effort to be taller. Mandy laughed at her and then quickly covered her mouth.

When called on, Donna answered, "to forgive our debts," carefully pronouncing the "b" and then the "t" at the end.

She was right and we all followed suit answering questions with superior knowledge of our Chapter. We were ready to compete at last!

* * * * *

The next two weeks flew by with school, volleyball practice, church and chores.

I barely had time to think about my feelings for Skip. I would see him pass by the gym on his way out to the football field and during science class but that was it. During the Homecoming assembly he sat directly behind me in the bleachers and laid his chin on my right shoulder.

"Want to lean back?" he asked.

I knew that meant we were going out even though it wasn't really verbalized. All the girls leaned back against their boyfriends in the bleachers. It excited me to be a part of this new group and experience being known as a couple by other students.

If I were to be completely honest with myself I would have known that the relationship would never last. We didn't have the friendship connection, the intellectual conversations that I enjoyed with other boys was missing. It was a small school and very clear who had what talents, whether they were strong or smart or both. Skip was strong.

Without saying a word I leaned back and he immediately put his arms around in front of me, presenting me with his football jersey.

I turned around quickly and asked, "For me?"

He looked at me and answered, "If you want it, it's yours."

I answered by putting it on over my shirt. I felt comfortable and safe with his jersey on and, for the first time, I felt like I was a real part of the town.

All the girls were more interested in us as a couple and I could talk to other boys without their girlfriends being threatened. It was even different when we, as a couple, would talk with other couples...like there was a common link between us. I was being threaded into a community blanket by my connections. I didn't need my boyfriend to be smart as long as I felt secure and wanted.

"We are the Oilers! The mighty mighty Oilers!" we all chanted as our six cheerleaders showed us how hard they had worked on keeping us pumped up for the Homecoming game. The assembly was a chance for them to perform with our full attention and we gave it to them. We were a perfect audience and participated fully in the cheers. We had pride for our school, for our team and for them.

Donna was having new experiences of her own. She had a current crush on a boy named David and he finally had asked her to go steady. He had a brother that was a year older than me and both of them were popular with the girls because of their curly hair, nice smile and tight jeans. As I walked out of the gymnasium with my friends we started to cross the grounds to the adjacent building where our lockers were, when I saw Donna and David standing face to face. I didn't think twice about it since Donna had been kissing boys since kindergarten.

All of a sudden we all heard Donna yell, "Gross!"

I turned my head to see what had happened and if she needed help. Her hands were on her hips as she continued to yell.

"Gross! Why'd you stick your tongue in my mouth?! That's so gross!"

She was yelling and spitting on the ground while David's face turned a bright deep red. It was obvious that he had tried to French kiss her and painfully obvious that Donna was not too happy with the new technique. Everyone I was with started laughing, including David's brother who happened to be with us. Donna didn't care about the laughing but David looked like he had just seen a horror movie. She was disgusted and let him know it. She was spitting the rest of the day. Needless to say, they broke up.

I later discovered that David still had tobacco in his lip when he had tried to kiss Donna. It was okay that some of the boys chewed tobacco because it was really common in Wyoming but the girls expected the courtesy of it being removed before kissing. I was even dared to try chewing t'bacca for a dollar and, of course, I did it. That wasn't my biggest mistake. My biggest mistake was that I didn't think about the fact that I had braces on and that it would be 'all up in my grill'. I had spent over an hour that night trying to get the little specks of black out of my braces. The sick feeling from the tobacco was nothing compared to the nauseating feeling I had over the fear of getting caught.

We raced home after school to get ready for the Homecoming game. The floats were going to be displayed during half time. Dad and Cindy were going to the game as well so we knew we could stay for the entire game. They were the paramedics and had to stay by the ambulance during the game. It was a hard job and they were very committed to it.

I had the opportunity to see Dad in action the year before when he had to put an air splint on our quarterback after he had fractured his shin bone. It was sticking out of his skin and shattered. As the quarterback went into shock my Dad quickly gave him an IV with fluids and a shot of pain medication. He worked quickly and methodically. As he waited for the parents to come over he explained to me that it was a compound fracture and would be a difficult fracture to heal. His football season was over and that made me sad. I was proud of the work my Dad did and I listened intently as he explained air splints and signs of shock. He was always teaching us about medical conditions and how to treat them.

The Homecoming game was all that I had expected. It was getting crispy cold in the evenings and the hot chocolate felt good as I held it between my hands. I sat in the bleachers just long enough to drink it and then I was up, yelling at my team to "GO, FIGHT, WIN!!!!" I squinted as I scanned the line of defenders looking for Skip's number. Once I found him I would yell his number and then lose track of him again. Our freshmen were able to get in some playing time because our class was strong and dedicated. I was proud of them all for being able to keep up with the upper classmen. I looked down and saw Donna under the bleachers with her friends. She was trying to hook Mandy up with someone but I couldn't tell who it was. I couldn't keep track.

The crowd cheered and as I looked up I saw that we had made another touchdown. I didn't even realize our offense was on the field. The cheerleaders never stopped moving and the crowd was energized. Finally, it was half-time and our floats were brought out to the track. The freshman float was of an oil well with our school colors and silver streamers. We had animated it so the head moved up and down like a real one. It was beautiful as it moved down the track bobbing its head as if to say, "Yes, yes the freshmen rock". Our hard work was obvious and I smiled broadly as the freshman class representatives waved.

As the game came to an end we celebrated our win by cheering and hugging our team. The football players were grinning and still releasing their testosterone with loud whoops and hollers. Skip hugged me and I immediately gasped as his shoulder pad jabbed me in the throat.

"Are you going to Greg's later?" he asked.

Everyone was making plans to get together but that was where I was, once again, out of the loop. Dad and Cindy were putting away the medical supplies and I only had a few minutes before I had to head home.

"No, I can't," I said with great disappointment. "My Dad won't go for it."

I would miss out on all the fun. I wasn't allowed to go hang out at anyone's house or stay the night with anyone. Cindy quickly glanced at Skip and me talking and told me to go find Donna. Grandpa would give us a ride to the house. I thought to myself, how unfair it was that I was 14 years old and had to have my Grandpa take me home instead of being with my friends for an hour. I didn't voice my opinion freely with Dad and Cindy like I would have with my Mom. There was no freedom of speech in Dad's house. We were children that had to follow rules and not protest or we would be going against God. In my Mom's home there were seven of us living in a 3 bedroom home and we spoke our opinions freely. We performed talent shows, we danced and we argued…as individuals. Mom and Leroy didn't expect us to be silent and just obey. I knew Mom would understand my feelings and I missed her.

I quickly said goodbye to Skip and went immediately to the bleachers to find Donna kissing Ross. Well, at least she wasn't fornicating so I didn't have to worry about her bursting into flames. "Come on", I commanded a little too strongly. She looked at me in surprise and started to argue but noticed my sad face and decided against it. Grandpa was waiting by his truck and drove us the seven blocks home.

* * * * *

Grandpa John was a heavy set man with dark wavy hair. He always had a smile on his face and an arm full of hugs for us. While he was married to my Grandma Carolyn (I was named after her) they raised 5 boys and 1 girl. My Dad used to tell us stories of growing up in Florida and catching snakes for the Science Department at the local University…barefoot and shirtless. Grandpa was on the road a lot as a trucker so he missed out on many of my Dad's growing up years. It seems like he was trying to make up for lost time by coming to Wyoming and taking an interest in all the same things that my Dad was interested in. My Dad was a deputy and then Grandpa became a deputy. Dad was an EMT 2 for the ambulance and then Grandpa started driving the ambulance. Dad went to church every Sunday and then Grandpa tried to go at least a couple times a month. He didn't do so well in that area. Dad married someone more than 10 years younger than himself the second time around. Grandpa married someone that was at least 20 years younger the second time around.

I wondered if they realized how similar their lives had become. Even so, they were very different people. Grandpa immersed himself in the social side of life. He loved children and visiting. He was very outgoing and emotional. Grandpa cried when he was happy, which was quite a bit. My Dad never cried and seldom showed much emotion at all. He would sit on the couch with his feet crossed on the coffee table with his arm on the end of the couch. His left arm would be raised up, cupping his chin and left cheek so he could gnaw on the inside of his cheek. It was a habit that he had and it always meant he was deep in thought. His eyes would be far away and I always thought he might be on the verge of finding a cure for diabetes or heart disease or cancer. So intently, he would gnaw on that cheek that surely he must be breaking the DNA code or determining the purpose of life.

In the little time it took for Grandpa to drive us the seven blocks home and hug us goodnight my attitude changed. I could never be upset around Grandpa. He waited for us to get inside our house and wave before he left. Mom would have appreciated that.

Donna raced upstairs to call Mandy as I made my full circle around the living room, through the kitchen, across the music room to my bedroom. Sometimes I wished I could just climb through my window by the door. I thought being the only one with a bedroom on the first floor would give me a great opportunity to raid the pantry at night but the consequences of getting caught by Cindy were too much. I would be humiliated for my lack of willpower and we would have to pray about it.

I tried my hardest to follow Cindy's example but secretly wished for one of my Dad's "midnight snacks". He used to take out all of the cereals and mix them together in a huge soup bowl then add raisins, dates and nuts. Next he would sprinkle on the wheat germ to make it extra healthy and dribble honey on the top. As he created his concoction he would smack his lips and his face would transform into a little boy's expression of pure delight. Donna and I followed suit by creating our own artistic expression of the perfect midnight snack. Once we were done, Dad would do the honors while we stood at attention by pouring the milk in each of our bowls. The sounds of love floated to our ears...snap, crackle, CRUNCH, CRUNCH, CRUNCH! We couldn't wait for our cereal to quit talking. We were hungry! There was no sitting down for the midnight snack. That was a breakfast thing to do. The midnight snack could only be fully appreciated by standing in the kitchen exactly where you stood when the milk was poured. We proudly gave our midnight snack the respect it deserved. When we were finally finished Donna would wipe her mouth, using her entire arm as a stand-in napkin, then smile and exclaim, "Mighty tasty!" Then Dad would announce that it was time to get back to bed. We had no problem getting back to sleep with our bellies full. I knew those days were over.

It was still warm in my bedroom so I cracked open my window for some air. There was a slight breeze coming off the prairie. I could smell the dusty dryness of sage with the slightest hint of sweet hay. During this time of year any grass that did grow had turned a light brown and the ranchers were done harvesting their crops. There had been tornado warnings just south of Casper. Normally the tornado warnings subsided by the end of August but one had touched down in Laramie County on September 2nd, a testimony to the unpredictable seasons.

The thought of tornadoes brought back the memory of mine and Donna's first tornado warning experience back in August of 1979. We hadn't moved in with Dad yet but were visiting for the summer and Dad was in the process of rebuilding the house. There was a partial basement without a roof (or ceiling) and the old cellar was removed. Dad had Police Dispatch call us on the base radio because he was out in the county and had just seen a tornado touch down about 60 miles outside of town. Cindy was 50 miles away at work in Casper so Donna and I were the only ones home.

We heard our names over the base and ran over to it, just standing there listening for a minute. Our names belted out again but this time we were instructed to pick up the red phone. The red phone! Our mouths dropped as we stared at each other in disbelief. Then we jumped as the red phone rang. The red phone was ringing and it was for us! Finally, I answered it with a breathless hello. I couldn't remember any of the police codes like 10-4 or 10-20 so it was a relief when a woman's voice calmly asked if I was Carolyn.

"Your father wants you and your sister to quickly get under the big desks. There's a tornado heading that direction so you need to take cover okay honey?"

Her voice sounded nice and as I answered that we would do as she asked, I also wondered if she was a mom. I hung up the phone and told Donna that we needed to prepare for a tornado.

Quickly, we raced around and collected the most important items we could think of and settled under the two desks. Luckily, they were in an "L" shape so we could talk as we huddled there. We weren't afraid at all thanks to our age and lack of understanding of the danger. Instead, we were proud that we had grabbed our stuffed animals, Winnie the Pooh and Eeyore. We were even more impressed that we had thought to save the top of Dad and Cindy's wedding cake…that had to be important. Most of all, we felt brilliant for having the wherewithal to remember food, not just any food though. We each grabbed six chocolate pudding cups to ensure our survival. It didn't need to be prepared and it didn't even require a spoon. Then, to make sure our survival skills were keen we decided to practice eating one of the puddings while waiting for the 'all clear' from the base radio. We didn't have to wait long before Dad showed up to let us know the tornado had skipped town and the warning was over. He looked confused as we handed him the top of his wedding cake and licked the chocolate off our fingers.

There would be no storm tonight. As I lay in bed I tucked my arms up under my head and wondered what Skip was doing at that very moment. I wondered if he wondered about me. I wondered when we would have our first real kiss. I fell asleep wondering about everything.

* * * * *

I spent Saturday morning wishing that Skip would call me but I knew he wouldn't take the chance. Donna and I weren't allowed to call boys so I thought I would have to wait until Monday to talk to him. I completely underestimated Donna's ability to play cupid.

"Wanna stay the night at Mandy's with me?" she asked.

I was surprised that she had asked me since I had never shown an interest.

"Nah, but thanks anyway," I responded. I was sure she was just feeling sorry for me.

"Skip will be staying the night with Jerry," she sang to me.

Jerry was Mandy's brother. Donna had a bit of a crush on him, being a boy and all. Suddenly I made the connection. Skip had worked it out so he could stay the night with Jerry! If I went with Donna then I would be able to talk to Skip all night!

"Yes! I'll go but what about Dad?" I worried.

"He won't know nothin'," Donna beamed. "We'll pretend we don't know and that he just showed up cuz we were already stayin' with Mandy and we didn't know nothin' about what Jerry was doing, no way, no how!" Donna explained.

She had already planned it all out…in the name of love! We knew that Dad and Cindy would let both of us go since they liked Mandy and figured that her parents wouldn't let us get into trouble. We would be able to walk to church in the morning since Mandy lived in Edgerton, just about 10 blocks from the church.

Once we arrived at Mandy's house I met her parents but quickly forgot them while I scanned the room for Skip. Jerry and Skip weren't there yet. I went to Mandy's room with Donna, plopped down on the bottom bunk and looked at all her posters. They lay on Mandy's floor with the yearbook open. The seconds passed by like years as I half listened to them talk about the drooling quality of every single boy they knew. I took it all in stride because I was truly grateful for their plan to get Skip and me together. To them, we were like Romeo and Juliet.

Suddenly we heard the door slam and heavy steps coming down the hall toward Jerry's bedroom. Donna and I looked at each other with the same expression of excitement.

"The boys are back!" Mandy happily exclaimed.

Now that they were actually in the house I became nervous. What would I say? What should I do? I had no time to figure it out as Mandy's bedroom door frame filled in with skin-tight muscle. He was wearing shorts and a half shirt with little holes in it. In one jump Skip was on the top bunk looking down at me with a smile. After I got over the fear of the top bunk collapsing onto the bottom bunk I smiled back. Life could not get any better than this! Quickly, Donna grabbed Mandy's arm and dragged her toward the door, "Come on, Mandy! Let's go see your brother!"

In an instant they were gone and I was alone with Skip.

"I missed you. Did you miss me?" Skip asked as he tucked himself under the bottom of the top bunk and flipped to the floor.

His face was only a few inches from mine as he kneeled next to the bed I was on and grabbed my hand. I inhaled quickly as he looked directly into my eyes, then looked at my lips and touched them with his finger. He waited for my response. What was the question?

"Huh?" I asked feeling a little embarrassed that I couldn't understand English anymore.

"I said," he began again; "I missed you. Can I kiss you?"

"Yes," I gulped.

My hearing was replaced with a pounding echo of my heart as I closed my eyes. With two of my senses shut down I could smell his cologne. I felt like I might faint. Within a millisecond I felt his breath on my skin just above my upper lip and then the full pressure of his lips touching mine. My blood was racing now. It was if my red blood cells were doing flips. I was surprised at how soft his lips were. He pulled away just long enough to look in my eyes again then went in for a 2nd kiss. This time he parted his lips and I knew it was going to be a French kiss. His tongue touched mine and it wasn't at all like Donna had experienced. The kiss left me breathless, not realizing I could breathe while kissing. We were interrupted on our 3rd kiss as Jerry came in the room looking for Skip. Jerry made some comment that I didn't quite understand and Skip went running out after him.

The rest of the night was a blur. There was no more kissing which was a good thing. My head was numb and I felt so giddy I didn't think I could take another kiss. We each stayed in our separate rooms but it was nice to think of him just on the other side of the wall. I slept well and the next morning he was already gone. As we walked to the church I told Donna that I owed her for making the kiss happen. She said I didn't owe her anything. She just loved seeing people in love and it gave her more time to see Jerry.

In the distance I saw Dad's bronco in front of the church. He was on duty so he and Cindy weren't together. He was leaning against the bronco talking to Christy. I was surprised that she was going to the morning service. She liked to sleep in and usually only showed up for Youth Group. Dad stood up straight when he saw us and I waved to him. When we reached them Donna gave Dad a big hug and Christy walked with me into the church.

"I'm surprised you are here so early," I told her.

"I needed to talk to Ed about some things that are going on," she confided, "I can't really talk about it."

It was weird to hear her call my Dad by his name.

"Okay, well I hope he can help you," I replied.

"He always does," she insisted.

* * * * *

My freshman classes at Midwest High were pretty basic with five core classes and one elective. The teachers were all very unique in personality and expectations so it was important to be flexible with them.

First period was Algebra which was a rude awakening to my brain first thing in the morning. I later learned that if I showed up early and played basketball in the gym before class started that I could concentrate much better. It was easy to show up early since I only drank coffee for breakfast now and Skip was always there. My Algebra teacher was a bit strange and I wondered why she chose to teach in a town that was so small and dusty. She had black short hair and pale skin with a large nose. The most interesting thing about her was that she wore Tonka toys around her neck. There were about six wooden blocks shaped like cars on a thick piece of yarn. It must have meant something important since she wore it every day. Maybe she had only been offered a job in Midwest because other teachers wouldn't drive so far. Whatever the reason, she was a great teacher and I learned to take a lot of notes in her class.

Second period I had History with Mr. Olson. Mr. Olson told us that if we slept with our History books under our pillow at night the information would actually leak up into our brain. I'm sure a few of my classmates tried it too. Mr. Olson was especially fond of the girls and extra mean to the boys.

After History I went to Art class as my elective. My Art teacher, Mrs. Hayes, was a hippie with long brown hair and huge glasses. She was long and slender with a gangly ostrich sort of posture. She made us listen to the same Bread record over and over every single day. She would sing the entire time as we sculpted heads, drew landscapes, painted ceramics and created wire masterpieces. Mrs. Hayes was also the volleyball coach but kept her two identities completely separate as if she were schizophrenic.

Fourth period I had Mr. Perkins for Science. Mr. Perkins had rheumatoid arthritis which caused him severe pain. We respected him for continuing to teach and learned more than Science in his class. He looked like a lion with red afro hair and a bushy beard. He called us all by our last names. The entire freshman class took Science, History, English and PE together as core requirements. In Science I sat next to Greg Hoff in the back row. We competed against each other for grades as an unspoken rule. Greg was late to class so I decided to play a prank on him and placed a thumbtack on his chair. I was sure he would notice it but when he came in he plopped (not sat) right onto the tack. He immediately screamed and I thought Mr. Perkins would surely make me go to the Principal's office.

"Mr. Hoff! Please sit down!"

Greg's face was red and he was furious.

"She put a tack on my chair!" he yelled in response.

"Mr. Hoff, sit down or leave this class!" Mr. Perkins demanded.

I couldn't believe it and neither could Greg. I didn't get in trouble and I was pretty sure Mr. Perkins was working very hard at not having a smile on his face. I had total respect for that man.

Fifth period we all had English. Mr. Anderson was very strict and straight laced. Again, Greg and I sat by each other and competed for every grade. Mr. Anderson also called us by our last names which I hated because he had more of a sarcastic tone in his voice. He announced to the class that the student with the highest grade point average in his class would receive an award and certificate. Greg looked at me and pointed to his chest. I returned his gesture by sticking out my tongue.

Sixth period was P.E. and a chance to sweat out all the boredom from English. P.E. also included swimming as a requirement on Tuesday and Thursdays. However, on this special day we all had to watch a Health film on reproduction. Everyone, boys and girls as well as freshmen and seniors, had to sit on the gym floor and watch the film from the 1970's that met the State requirements but neglected to show anything at all worth watching. I looked for Christy but she wasn't there so I sat by Amy.

As I lay on the gym floor I started feeling really sick to my stomach so I ran into the girl's locker room. I started my period unexpectedly and the cramps were bad. There was a lot of blood and I didn't have anything to wear for protection. As I sat on the toilet I felt my skin getting cold and moist. I was going to faint. I knew this because I started menstruating when I was eleven years old and only in the 6th grade. My cramps could get so bad that I would fall and not be able to walk. I fainted a lot and my Mom had spent many nights up with me as I suffered through the pain. But here I was in the girl's locker room by myself and ready to faint. I controlled my breathing and rolled up a wad of toilet paper to put in my underwear. I leaned back against the toilet tank and fainted. It was brief but I knew I had to get out of there. The blood hadn't soaked through my jeans and it was dark in the gym so no one would notice. I walked out and told my teacher I was sick and was going to the nurse. There was no doubt about it since my face was white and sweaty. The teacher asked Amy to walk me to the nurse which was a great idea since I was feeling faint again. The pain was unbearable and I doubled over in agony twice before making it to the nurse.

When I told the nurse what was going on she gave me a hot water bottle to place on my abdomen. It didn't help at all but she kept insisting that I use it. Finally, in frustration, I threw it across the room. She took the hint and came over with the thermometer. She determined that I had a fever of 101 degrees and should go home. She called my house several times but there was no answer. My Dad was off so he normally would be home. I assured her that I could walk home and that my Dad would be there. She agreed as she reached down to pick up the hot water bottle but I don't think it was because she thought my Dad was home.

I walked the eight blocks home, stopping periodically to breathe as the cramps coursed down my legs. I was full of doubt and wondered if I should have left the nurse. It seemed like a long way home and I wished I would have thought to ask the nurse to send Donna with me.

As I walked past the front of my house I could hear music. Dad was home after all! I was relieved to know I wouldn't be alone and wiped the sweat off my face. I walked into the house and went around the living room, through the kitchen, through the music room, into my bedroom and finally my bathroom. Once I was cleaned up I went to find Dad but I didn't have far to go. He was in the music room looking for some different music.

Apparently, I startled him because he jumped back and asked what I was doing there. I started to explain that I was sick as he quickly turned off the music. He asked me why I couldn't tough it out and why the nurse didn't keep me there. I was speechless and unprepared to answer the questions, having no understanding of why it didn't make sense to him that I had come home. Before I could answer he said that since I was sick enough to come home from school that I could just stay in bed the rest of the night.

Five minutes later he announced that he had some errands to run and left the house. I cried for a long time after he left. I lay in my bed, sick, in pain and lonely.

A storm was brewing.

Chapter 5

Secrets & Visions

Autumn passed by in a blur of activity as winter barreled across the prairie and settled in for a long visit. The tumble weeds had tumbled away and the townspeople were making plans for the hunting season. Skip and I had been together for 2 months and I expected us to go steady until we graduated. He gave me his class ring which I wore faithfully at school. I still didn't feel right about advertising our relationship around Dad and Cindy but I loved showing off his ring at school.

Wrestling season had started so I spent all my extra time at the school during the matches. Skip was a great wrestler. His facial expressions were intense as the veins bulged in his forearms. He exploded from the down position, quickly paralyzing his opponent in the cradle position. It was rare that he needed the full 3 minutes. Once I caught on to the positions and how the tournaments worked it was fun to watch all the wrestlers.

Amy and a group of girls sat together in the far right upper corner of the bleachers. They were exceptionally loud during one of the tournaments and I went over to say hi and see what was so exciting. Amy had a clear bottle with red liquid in it and happily handed it to me. I took a big gulp and all the girls laughed hysterically as I realized it was Cinnamon Schnapps that I had just drunk. My mouth was on fire! My throat was melting! My whole body was on fire! I made such a commotion that the wrestlers and coaches looked our way. All I could do was stand there looking embarrassed...which was perfect since my cheeks were bright red from the Schnapps.

I was amazed at how quickly a wrestler could lose pounds to qualify for a weight class and asked Skip after the match to tell me his secret. When he told me that he drank raw eggs, I cringed as my stomach flipped. However, the desire to lose weight fast and easy was too much for me to resist so I tried it the next Saturday. Donna was present to witness my heroic attempt, as well as to make unnecessary gagging noises. I placed the tall glass on the counter and cracked two eggs into it, being careful not to drop any shells. The egg whites slowly poured out until the gravity of the yolk quickly forced the thick mass, all at once, to plop into the bottom of my glass.

Donna scrunched up her nose and then laughed until I stared her down with my evil eye. She quickly stopped laughing for fear of losing her front row seat to my weight-loss experiment. I had neglected to ask Skip whether I should stir the eggs together or not. I decided that I would not mix them and that way I could swallow one at a time and keep the yolk from breaking. Taking a deep breath I lifted the glass to my mouth. The raw eggs quickly glided down, to my horror, at the same time and into my mouth. I swallowed several times before the thick, snot textured eggs went completely down. Donna was in complete awe that I had actually followed through with the plan but that didn't make me feel any better. No sooner did I set the empty glass on the counter that I could feel the eggs coming back up. I ran to my bathroom and spent a full hour vomiting into the toilet. Apparently, Skip had forgotten to tell me how the raw eggs worked to help him lose the weight. I had assumed the protein was the reason. I had assumed wrong.

* * * * *

The winter wind and longer nights meant Donna and I had to spend more time indoors which we found to be extremely boring. The snow hadn't really made an entrance so we were in a state of wait. One Saturday we were so bored that we couldn't even watch television.

Donna and I slumped on the loveseat upstairs in front of the TV. An old episode of Taxi was on but it wasn't enough to pull us out of our stupor.

"I'm so bored," Donna complained.

"I'm bored too," I replied.

"No, I'm so bored I can't move my legs," Donna whined.

"I'm so bored I can't move my eyes," I stated very slowly.

"Well...I...can....hardly...move...my...mouth..."Donna mumbled.

We were like jello, slowly sinking deep into the furniture as if it were quicksand swallowing us up. It took a good twenty minutes to build up any motive to move but even at our most boring moment ever, we had enough energy to laugh and entertain each other.

During the weekdays after school we found ways to entertain ourselves as well. I especially loved to scare Donna whenever possible. I had it down to a science. One afternoon she was focused on carrying the upstairs garbage down to the kitchen garbage can which required her to make several right turns in the house. I crouched down on the other side of a turn, patiently waiting. I jumped out at her from down by the floor instead of from a standing position. The results were more magnificent than I had ever expected! She threw the little garbage can up over her head, flinging the contents all over the living room. Then she dropped to the floor, kicking her legs and flailing her arms while she screamed in horror. "Donna! It's me!" I yelled then burst out into a long side-wrenching spell of laughter.

Donna recovered and joined me in my glee. Finally, we calmed down and she looked at me seriously, "You hafta help me pick up the garbage."

Donna and I helped out more with dinner during the evenings when Cindy worked late. Cindy thought it would be a good idea to take our cooking abilities to the next level and left us with instructions for making mashed potatoes. I went first with great confidence. I had watched my Mom make mashed potatoes with the metal handled mashing tool and looked forward to annihilating some boiled potatoes. I used a fork to test the doneness of the potatoes. The fork slid through each potato with ease so I drained out the water and placed the starchy veggies in a big bowl for mashing. Slowly, I applied pressure to the metal potato masher and watched in delight as long squares of potatoes formed like worms coming out of the ground. I grabbed the butter from the fridge and plopped in a big spoonful. I then decided that I could never have too much butter so I added two more spoonfuls.

As the butter melted over the steaming potatoes I slowly poured in the milk. I knew the milk was the secret to a creamy texture so I made sure to add twice the amount that Cindy normally added. Dad would be so impressed at dinner time and shocked to discover my hidden culinary talent! Donna watched as I finished mixing the potatoes into a creamy thin paste. Something didn't seem quite right but I decided that maybe I was just being a perfectionist. Donna grabbed the chicken from the microwave. Cindy had prepared it the night before so we could just heat and serve.

Dad was already waiting at the table we had set. Donna carefully carried the chicken platter to the table. I followed with the mashed potatoes and placed the bowl right in front of Dad's plate. Once Donna and I sat down Dad said a prayer thanking God for my mashed potatoes and the entire meal. Actually, he didn't mention the potatoes in the prayer but I knew that he would be especially thankful once he sampled them. Donna and I were happy to see Dad lick his lips and rub his hands together. As he spooned the mashed potatoes on his plate the smile on his face quickly turned up-side down. The contents in the spoon poured out onto his plate like soup.
"Who made this?" he asked while placing the spoon back in the bowl.
My face turned red as I admitted to being the one responsible for the liquid pouring from his plate and onto the table.
"What were you thinking?" he asked with a slightly disgusted look on his face.
Tears swelled in my eyes as I swallowed hard, trying not to give them up to my cheeks.
"Donna, give me the chicken," he instructed.
Donna looked at me sympathetically and passed over the platter. I vowed never to mash potatoes again.

The next day Donna made the potatoes. She had learned from my mistakes a little too well. Again we sat at the table. Again Dad went for the mashed potatoes. He took a large spoonful and instead of the potatoes pouring onto his plate they refused to come off the spoon. Donna's potatoes were so thick and sticky that they wouldn't budge. Donna glanced at me with round eyes and we braced for the verbal lashing to come. Dad scraped the potatoes from the spoon with his fork then looked at both of us and smiled, then laughed.

"Well, it looks like you've corrected the soup problem."

Donna and I both laughed in relief and I announced that next time we would both make the potatoes and then they would be perfect.

* * * * *

The holidays in Wyoming were very different from what I was used to in Washington. Thanksgiving looked the same on the surface, with the feast fit for a king and the family sitting at the table saying a Thanksgiving prayer but that's where the similarities ended.

At my Mom's, we sub-consciously paced through the kitchen and living room making comments about how we were so close to starvation that we didn't think we could make it another minute. When it was time for Leroy to lift the turkey out of the oven for carving, Mom would yell at us all to get out of the kitchen while she mashed potatoes. This yell also served as our version of ringing the dinner bell. The kitchen was small but had an opening on each end so you could circle in and out. For a family of seven, this design was perfect because we could line up at one end, make our way through the kitchen filling our plates buffet style and sit down at the table on the other end. Genius! Leroy said the prayer then we all dug in.

At my Dad's, Donna and I set the table with the good china and "real" silverware after putting down the lace table cloth. We couldn't figure out why we needed so many forks when one fork worked just fine. Then we set out the crystal glasses. Donna made flowers out of the cloth napkins as I placed the butter dish and salt and pepper in the middle of the table next to the candle holders. Everything had to be in its proper place, including us.

We changed into our Sunday clothes which, for me, meant white slacks over nylons and a sweater. My nylon crotch didn't fit right and stretched tight about mid-thigh which was about as comfortable as my wool sweater scratching at my neck. Instead of eating buffet style, all the trimmings were placed in fancy bowls and on the table. The turkey was resting on the platter that's only purpose was to be a turkey platter. Once Dad was ready we were allowed to sit down. Dad's prayer was much longer than Leroy's and I would feel the heat from my nylons and sweater getting the best of me. Finally, we would all say "Amen" and watch Dad carve the turkey with an electric knife.

* * * * *

Thanksgiving had passed and Christmas was quickly approaching. Cindy was busy planning her Christmas goodie basket lists, making quilts for the holiday bazaar and visiting with her close friend Jenny. Donna and I decided to go on a hay ride and sing Christmas carols. The snow had already paid a brief visit so the hay ride took on a magical Christmas card look as the truck and flatbed came by our house. We rushed to the roadside and jumped on, taking our place amongst the hay bales. Everyone was smiling and singing! Before we knew it, we had sheet music in our hands and were singing *Joy to the World* at the top of our lungs.

The snow was dry compared to the wet stuff we were used to in Washington. It blew around like dandelion seeds, restless, not wanting to settle down quite yet. The small flakes blew into our hair, hanging on for a moment before letting go to dance on the wind. We were mesmerized by the circles and loops. It was as if the dancing snow was creating its own sheet of music right before our eyes. Our eyes interpreted the music as our hearts became instruments of peace.

It was natural for Donna and me to love snow, all snow. As soon as the first flake of the season fell we would jump up and down, yelling "Snow! Snow! Snow!" The more the merrier! We had experienced snow in Alaska that went as high as the 2nd story on our Grandma's house so huge amounts of snow didn't scare us. It made our minds go crazy with the possibilities!

When we woke up last winter to find 9 foot snow drifts in the middle of our streets we went wild. Never had we seen such a sight. The wind had been busy while we were asleep, sculpting huge snow drifts that looked like the soft serve ice-cream from Dairy Queen. We could see the black road surface for a couple yards and then bam! a huge snow drift. Some cars were completely snow-free while others were invisible under the drifts. Donna and I slowly walked up to the closest snow drift and began to survey its structural integrity. We both knew that it would be a perfect igloo and started planning where our entrance would be when we heard someone yelling from the other side. It was a couple of neighbor boys, both Donna's age, encouraging us to come over and play with them. Just as we started to tell them we had plans one of the boys sprinted toward a snow drift and dove head first right into the middle of it. His body went in half way before stopping. All we could see were his butt and legs dangling from the snow drift. After laughing until our stomachs ached we realized he really was stuck and his friend was too small to pull him out. Donna and I ran over and grabbed a leg, pulling him to safety before going into another laughing fit. We couldn't tell if his face was red from snow burn or embarrassment.

I didn't know if this winter would bring about snow drifts, I would have to wait and see. I did know the dangers of snowstorms on the prairie and prayed that no one would be caught out in one. During the last winter Dad and a group of volunteers had searched for a pregnant woman out on the prairie in the middle of a white-out. The wind was wicked and the temperature was at a dangerous level. We knew it as 30-30-30 which meant -30 degrees with a 30 mph wind and you will have frost bite on any exposed skin within 30 seconds. They never found the woman. Dad told us that he thought it had only been a rumor but we had a feeling that he was sparing us from the tragedy. We didn't dwell on it though and made a mental decision to believe his story without questioning it. It was easier to believe than to doubt…and less painful.

* * * * *

Christmas break meant staying the night with friends. The Quiz Show competitions were postponed until mid-January so we didn't have to study for school or church. Donna and Mandy had already planned back to back overnights with each other and were busily memorizing phone numbers of all the boys they knew when Christy called. She wanted me to stay the night. I was surprised but excited at the same time since I had never stayed at her place and Dad agreed to drive me over since he was heading to Grandpa John's house down the road anyway.

As soon as I walked into Christy's house her three sisters barreled down the stairs to greet me. They all escorted me around their house which took about two minutes and then ushered me up the narrow stairway to their room. They all shared one big room which was the entire upstairs space. Each section was clearly marked by personal belongings, a twin bed and tape across the floor. Christy's bed was next to the window that overlooked the street but she informed me that we would be sleeping in the living room on the sofa bed so we could talk in peace. It didn't matter to me where I slept. I was happy to stay upstairs too but I could sense that privacy was a real issue with these sisters.

Christy and I made the couch out into a bed we started talking about whatever came to mind. I knew Christy was experienced with the boys so I started asking her about making out. I described to her my technique for French kissing and that I thought moving my tongue clock-wise was way more intense than just being random. She looked at me like I had lost my mind then laughed gently like a teacher with a new student. She asked me how far I had gone with Skip and was surprised that we hadn't made it past the kissing stage. I asked her to tell me about her experiences and she blushed...then I blushed when I discovered that she had gone all the way.

Christy had been having sex for a couple years. In light of this ominous news I tried to grasp the meaning of what I had just heard. I knew that she smoke cigarettes, had smoked pot before and that she also drank alcohol but this was much more than that. I asked her who she had slept with and she started naming names of boys I knew in school. I was shocked but I was also curious. She explained that while she didn't like sleeping around she had a hard time telling certain boys no. That made me feel protective and I told her to call me if that happened again and I would help talk her out of it.

Our conversation had silenced us so I decided to lighten things up and asked, "What is a blow job?" Christy choked on her own spit which made me laugh.
"I mean...how do you do it? Do you really blow on it?" I continued.
Christy sat up in the bed, laughed and then smiled broadly.
"I'll tell you but you can't let Ed know I was talking to you about this or he will never let you stay the night again!"
I frowned, "Why would I tell my Dad? He doesn't even know I French kiss. Besides, I'm not going to do it. I just want to know what it is. Please!"
Christy proceeded to give me the finer details of a blow job and when she was done I was completely and utterly disgusted.
"Why would you ever want to do that?" I asked.
"Well", she confided, "they love it and it's not like having sex or anything so when they ask I figure, why not?"
I wasn't convinced but I was done asking questions, mostly because I was afraid to hear the answers. Just as we faded off to sleep I whispered, "Christy?"
She was still awake. "What?"

"I hope you can say no next time…it's fornicating you know?"

She was silent for a moment and then whispered, "I hope so too."

* * * * *

It was two weeks before Christmas when we tip-toed down the basement stairs to see our gifts, unwrapped, scattered all over the floor around an exercise bench. Christy had stopped by earlier in the afternoon and Dad invited her to go down and check out our gifts. After 30 minutes Christy walked back into the living room with a big smile on her face.

"I know what you got for Christmas!" she cheered.

I was not happy at all. It was bad enough that she was rubbing it in, but now I couldn't call her and brag about it on Christmas day because she would already know.

"I don't care." I grumbled and walked away.

I didn't even wait to find out why she had stopped by.

Later that day, I told Donna that we should go down and peek at our presents since they really weren't a secret now that Christy knew about them. I didn't have to convince her much and the next thing I knew we were standing at the bottom of the stairs looking at beige low heeled shoes for me and black no heeled shoes for Donna. There were jackets, gloves and boots too. We didn't take another step toward the gifts. Instead, I was frozen in my own guilt and shame for breaking the rules. Slowly we turned around and, without a single word, crept back up the steps. We would never do that again.

Christmas morning finally arrived. As Donna and I sat close to the tree Dad and Cindy went to the kitchen to pour fresh coffee into their mugs. Donna and I looked at each other with guilt ridden faces. We knew what was in each and every package. It was going to be very important for us to show surprise and excitement as we opened each gift without going overboard and giving our secret away. It was at this moment we both realized how foolish we had been to give into temptation.

My jacket turned out to be part of a ski suit with gray matching bibs. I didn't know how to ski but I would definitely stay warm and dry walking to and from school. There were a few gifts we had not seen after all, maybe last minute purchases, so the guilt fell away like the wrapping paper from our gifts and the natural excitement of Christmas overcame our shame.

* * * * *

Donna and I wore our new jackets and boots to school expecting to stand out from the crowd but instead, we faded into the background along with all the other students that received new jackets for Christmas. The halls were electrified with the static of Christmas vacation stories and basketball players bounding down the hall toward the gym for practice. Donna and I both agreed that the best thing about basketball was that the boys wore shorts and tank tops. Skip stopped by my locker in his maroon shorts and a black net top that only covered the top part of his chest.

"Hey, are you going to stay for the game?" he asked.

I had forgotten about the game and hadn't planned to stay.

"I can't", I frowned, "I forgot and I have homework in Algebra."

He was disappointed so I quickly reminded him, "We are going on that field trip to Thermopolis in two-weeks so be sure to come to Youth Group Sunday so you can go."

That was enough to get him smiling again. He quickly kissed my cheek and ran off after Greg. The only way I was going to get Skip to go to church was to bribe him with a field trip to a natural hot springs resort in Thermopolis and I was more than happy to do it.

Homework started to become more challenging and consumed a lot of my time after school. Donna didn't seem to ever have homework unless you count socializing as a subject. As I sat at the dining room table with algebraic equations strewn all over the place, Donna and Mandy discovered a cabinet full of alcohol. There were at least 8 bottles of alcohol, everything from vodka and whiskey to rum and gin. They lined up the bottles on the kitchen counter and started reading the labels. I knew that Donna wouldn't drink one of them because the punishment wouldn't be worth it and surely Dad would notice a missing bottle. I turned back toward my homework, completed my math and pulled out my English Comp assignment.

Just as I was finishing the first paragraph of my essay, Donna and Mandy both bumped into the table, fell to the ground and started laughing hysterically. I had completely underestimated my sister. Instead of drinking from one bottle they had drunk a small portion from each bottle. These *fractions* added up to much more than a *whole* according to my calculations and the laughing *proof* was rolling around on the floor.

"Donna!" I yelled, "Cindy is going to be home in a half hour and you are going to be in BIG trouble!" Slowly, Donna got to her knees, leveled her eyes to the edge of the table like a crocodile and said, "Don't be such a Goody-Two-Shoes!" This sent them both into a laughing fit so I quickly gathered my homework, told Donna she was retarded and stomped off to my room.

By the time Cindy walked into the house everything was spic and span and back in its place. Luckily for Donna, Cindy had planned to go visit her friend Jenny and never suspected that Donna's uncontrollable giggles were anything more than just plain goofiness.

* * * * *

It was still dark when we arrived at the church for the big field trip to Thermopolis. Everything, birds and bugs, were still asleep and the silence was so pronounced that it seemed as though the end had come and somehow we had missed it. Every movement echoed. I could hear Donna zipping her jacket and Mandy shuffling her feet on the other side of the church van. Christy walked the block from her house to the church without anyone noticing her until she was right beside my Dad. Our minds were still groggy as we loitered around the van waiting for the rest of our group. My heart jumped when I heard someone running down the street. It was Skip! He made it! I quickly glanced at Christy as she gave me a knowing smile. I then turned to look at my Dad's response but there was nothing. He either didn't know about Skip and I or he was not interested.

Finally, everyone was accounted for and we all piled into the 15-passenger van. Christy was the first to climb in. She saved the back seats for us and I instantly felt like I had overdosed on caffeine. I was giddy with excitement. The back seat was a bench seat and it went all the way across the van. My heart was racing as I sat next to Skip and kissed him. My smile was so big that I thought my cheeks might burst. As I looked up to the front of the van I could see my Dad in the driver's seat looking in the rearview mirror right at me. I tried to wipe the smile off my face but I couldn't. I knew that I should be focused on saving Skip's soul from the burning depths of Hell but...well...his aftershave was way too hypnotic for me to do that right now. By the look on Dad's face there was no doubt that he had seen the kiss but I didn't care. He wouldn't be able to say anything until we were back home and that wouldn't be for at least twelve glorious hours.

The van was warm so when I stepped out into the parking lot of the Thermopolis hot springs park, the crisp cold winter air took my breath away. A cement block building was shrouded in wisps of white steam and I could smell mild sulfur in the air, as if someone had lit a match. We ran toward the building and discovered that it was much larger than it first appeared. There were locker rooms and two indoor swimming pools. One was a standard Olympic size pool with a high dive and the other was three times that size with slides. There was a huge glass wall that was partially opened so you could actually go from the slide pool to an outdoor pool without going through a door. It was so steamy that my mind wasn't always convinced that I was actually seeing things right. I wondered if this was how people saw things when they were high.

Once we had our swim suits on, we met by the high dive. We were all expert swimmers since swimming was a PE requirement at the school. Even my Dad was excited to get into the medicinal pools and dove right in. I dove in after him and was surprised at the warmth and softness of the water. With my right hand I combed back my hair and wiped the water from my face. As I looked around all I could see was the white steam rising. It was as if I were swimming in the ocean at night as fog lay thick on its surface.

All of a sudden I heard, "Marco....Polo....Marco" all around me. No one had to cover their eyes to play this game! As I squinted my eyes a face started to form in the white curtain in front of me. It was Donna.
"Isn't this awesome?" she yelled, as if not seeing anything meant that I couldn't hear anything.
I was excited too and yelled back, "This is sooo cool! Have you found anyone else yet?"
"No", she replied, "but I keep yelling Polo just for fun even tho I'm not playing! I'm gonna go find Boogs now. See ya!"
Boogs was Mandy's nickname. As Donna drifted back into the white steam I could hear her yelling Polo and then someone else yelled back at her that they knew she wasn't on the team. She had been discovered.

Just as I had given up on finding anyone else, a breeze momentarily lifted the steam away from the outdoor slide where

Skip was standing. Once I made it over to the slide, I climbed the short ladder out of the pool and went to the ladder for the slide. It was bitter cold outside but my body was still warm from the hot springs. I smiled at Skip as I grabbed the side of the ladder. The warm, moist skin of my hand stuck to the frozen metal immediately.

"It's stuck!" I yelled in horror.

Before Skip could reply my Dad ran from the pool and splashed my hand with more water, freeing it from the ladder.

"It's safer if you dry your hands first," he advised as he quickly climbed the ladder himself and flew down the slide.

He was having way more fun than I was so I rushed up the ladder, down the slide and swam after him until I was riding on him piggy back. I felt like his little girl again! He grabbed my hands and took me under water with him. I held my breath as long as I could, which ended up being a split second too short. As I hacked up the water from my lungs Dad said something about learning to hold my breath longer and swam away. Normally, I would have been upset but I remembered who my guest was and smiled.

I spent the rest of the afternoon with Skip, running from slide to slide, indoors and outdoors. Our athletic bodies never slowed down and we took full advantage of the time in the pools. Christy didn't run around at all but spent most of her time in a corner of the pool. She wasn't very athletic and seemed to always be waiting for something. Donna and Mandy made friends with everyone and were finally part of the *Marco Polo* team for real. I knew it had only been a matter of time. On the way home we were all exhausted and I slept with my head on Skip's shoulder all the way back to the church.

Dad didn't say a word about the kiss and the distance that had been growing between us was nurtured in the silence.

* * * * *

My Dad loved parables so when Rev. Dewey asked him to present a sermon to the congregation I wasn't surprised when he chose the Dog and the Bone parable. I wasn't sure where it came from, whether he made it up or read it somewhere but it wasn't the author that mattered as much as the message.

"There once was a man walking down a city block. As he crossed in front of an alley he glanced down the dark, damp street and saw a starving stray dog standing amongst garbage that had been whipped up and strewn along one side of a building. The man was curious and stopped to see what the dog had in its mouth. As the dog cowered in fear, the man recognized the dried up old bone clenched between the dogs decaying teeth. The man knew that this dog was going to die of starvation if he didn't act soon. He went straight to the local butcher and purchased the biggest, most succulent steak he could find.

Wasting no time, he quickly returned to the alley to save the dog from its fate. Slowly, the man stepped toward the dog. In return, the dog growled severely and backed away. The man held the juicy steak up before the dog and spoke softly. Very gingerly the dog approached the man, its eyes dull and sunken. The man became hopeful as he laid the steak on the ground and backed away. The dog smelled the steak but would not drop the old bone. The man encouraged the dog but the dog held firm. The man thought that surely the dog would take the meat if he left so he went on home for the night.

The next day the man returned to the alley to find the dog lying in the alley next to the uneaten steak, dead. Slowly, the man walked up to the dog and noticed that the dried up bone was still clenched tightly between the dogs jaw. It was then that the man realized that the dog must have had that bone in its mouth for a long time. It was all the dog knew and all the dog could rely on in the world. Even with the promise of being saved, the dog held fast to what it knew to be true. If the dog released the bone would the steak still be there? Was the man tempting him or saving him? There was no way to be sure so rather than take the chance and accept salvation the dog accepted its fate and died a lonely death."

I thought this story was so sad and was not at all happy with the dog dying at the end. Trust was the key to this story. God has a plan for all of us and we need to trust that HE has our best interest in mind; that HE will not let us perish, that HE will nourish our starving souls. It is up to us to let go of our worldly possessions, to drop things from our lives that did not lead us toward salvation. I understood the point of the story but still felt bad about the dog.

It was mid-week when Donna and I came home after school to a surprise visitor. Reverend Dewey was sitting with our father in the living room. As soon as Dad saw us he placed his coffee mug on the end table as Rev. Dewey stood to greet us. "Come over here girls and sit down. Rev. Dewey and I have something we think you need to hear." Dad seemed concerned so we immediately sat down in the living room and directed our attention toward the Rev. As our pastor paced slowly back and forth across the living room carpet from his chair to the stone fireplace and back, I wondered why we were summoned before him. There was a strange silence from my Dad as I glanced at his face for any sign of what might have happened.

Rev. Dewey placed his right hand up to his chin and rubbed his cheek as he decided how to begin.
"Carolyn. Donna."
He pivoted toward us as he directed all his focus on the task at hand.
"I came here to speak with your father about a vision I had last night. We've discussed it at length and have agreed that the two of you need to hear about this vision as it pertains to you as well. I've told your father, and he agrees that this vision that came to me in a dream is a vision from God."
Donna didn't move a muscle and I knew she was awe struck too. Our very own pastor came to our humble home to tell us about a vision God gave him!
"In this dream your father was walking down railroad tracks. He continued to walk until he came to a switch. He had to choose a path."
Rev. Dewey turned toward our father, paused and then turned back to us and continued, "Anyway, that part of the dream has to be determined by your father. This dream...vision...had the two of you in it as well. You were both standing side by side and next to each of you were two human sized snakes standing upright as if they were human."
Rev. Dewey paused again, slowly turned back toward his chair and sat down.

Our pastor and our father sat silently for a moment so we could let this epiphany soak in. I wasn't sure exactly what the vision meant for my Dad but I was pretty sure the snakes had to be Satan. I couldn't imagine why there would be two snakes instead of one. As if reading my mind, my father stood and cleared his throat.

"Girls, this is serious but we don't want you to be afraid. This is a message from God to be careful. The snakes probably represent people in your life that can take you down the wrong path...such as boys...that's why you each have a snake. Do you understand?"

We both nodded without saying a word. Did they think Satan was using boys to lead us down the path to Hell? Donna and I both stood up as Dad gave us permission to go to our rooms and think about what we had just heard. As I turned the corner in the kitchen to my room I wondered if Dad thought Skip was somehow Satan's way of tempting me...the kissing...how I acted in the van...there was no doubt in my mind that I was tempted but my instincts told me that this vision from God had nothing to do with boys.

Chapter 6

FOG

Earth's natural Eraser
slowly Dissolving the Pastures
Leaving half Trees in its Wake.

Evening's soft Mist
Shushing birds under its Blanket
while Hanging Mountains on the Horizon.

Carolyn A. Ames

We were on our way home from the last Quiz Show for the year and the drive was a long one. The fog had been thick in places and had slowed our travelling time so it would be still another hour before we made it home into our beds. Our team had done well against the other church but not well enough to continue on in the competition. Still, we felt happy and knew that the most important thing was to learn the Bible verses and lessons.

I sat in the front of the car by the door, Christy was next to me in the middle and Dad drove. Donna and her two friends were fast asleep in the back snuggled together like puppies. We had gone from chattering a hundred miles per hour to a sleepy silence. Listening to Donna breathe heavily in the backseat asleep, I envied her ability to nap on these road trips. I had never been able to rest in a moving car, always afraid I might miss out on something.

Gradually, my mind started drifting as I watched for antelope eyes outside my window. It was bitter cold outside and toasty warm in the car. The dash lights glowed softly as my eye lids grew heavy against the weight of the day. The window was cold against the skin of my cheek as I rested my head at an awkward angle against the door. With eyes barely open I could still see the white fog line along the highway. Seconds blurred into minutes as my mind went on autopilot. I had learned the autopilot technique while traveling cross country from Florida to Alaska with my parents when I was barely six years old and it still worked for me at the age of fourteen...well, almost fifteen. I was half asleep, able to rest my mind and body but also able to be alert at a moment's notice if an owl swooped by or an antelope jumped from the wild onto the domestic highway.

Just as the last sliver of my consciousness began to fade, I sensed a movement to my left. Without moving a single muscle in my body I could use my peripheral vision to see that my Dad had placed his hand on Christy's knee. Assuming I must be dreaming I turned slightly so my vision would be clear. The next move I witnessed sent electricity through my nerves. My Dad's hand was clearly on Christy's knee and slowly sliding over her thigh. I could hear the skin of his palm on her jeans as the dash lights illuminated the back of his hand in a light green. Christy reciprocated by placing her left hand on his knee, moving it slowly up his thigh. My heart was pounding so hard that I could feel it in my ears and I thought they might hear it. Just as she slid her hand from the top of his thigh to his inner thigh and down between to his crotch she looked up to his face. He smiled and moved his hand to her crotch, rubbing it slowly. This was more than I could take and I elbowed Christy to let her know I was wide awake and completely aware of what was going on. All the blood drained from my best friend's face as she turned to see my piercing glare. Our eyes locked for a split second as I swallowed hard trying to keep down the bitter taste of betrayal. Quickly, she removed her hand from my Dad's zipper and grabbed his hand to make him stop. When he didn't take the hint she elbowed him and nodded her head toward me. I had already turned back to the cool window and the fog line which was now blurred by free-flowing tears. My sobs were silent as I forced them into internal anguish. There was no mistaking what I had witnessed, no story I could tell myself to make it go away.

We were almost to town when I decided that I wouldn't tell Donna. There was no sense in breaking her heart and maybe this was one temptation that only I would know about. Even a man like my father could be tempted to sin and maybe Christy started it. There were many teenage girls that had crushes on my father and it was obvious that she was one of them. Luckily I had stopped things from going too far. These thoughts settled my mind and my stomach as the lights of town appeared on the horizon. It was only a matter of minutes before we would be dropping off Christy and the other two girls. Then we would go the one mile home where Dad would realize what a mistake he had made just as I had made a mistake in my choice of friends.

Donna woke up in time to see the lights of town and ask if we were home yet. That woke the other two girls up and as they straightened out Dad announced that he would drop off Donna and I first. That didn't make sense at all so I spoke for the first time.

"Why not drop them off first? It's closer."

I was surprised when I heard the sarcasm in my voice. Did my Dad forget what I had just witnessed?

"You and your sister need to get to bed and I need to talk to Christy."

Dad's tone wasn't sarcastic at all. It was natural like everything was fine. I hoped that he was going to tell her that she could never call or come over and that she was going to hell unless she asked God for forgiveness.

As the Chrysler stopped in front of the house I jumped out and ran to the door. I stood with my back to the car, waiting for Donna to catch up.

"What's your hurry? Got a hot date?" Donna mumbled.

I didn't answer her, I couldn't. She was the one person that would be able to knock down the wall I was carefully building.

Cindy was still up sewing when we came in. "Where's your Dad?"

"He's taking the other girls home, then Christy."

I hadn't even thought about what Cindy would think and I wasn't about to be the one to tell her that her husband was being tempted at the very moment we were speaking.

"Why didn't he take them home first?"

Cindy was asking more to herself than to me but I answered anyway.

"I don't know."

With that, I turned and went to my bedroom so I could let the sobs seep into my pillow.

The exhaustion I felt kept me from crying too long as I dozed off. It was midnight when my phone rang.

"Hello?" It was Christy.

I remained silent, not wanting to talk to her, too angry to form a sentence.

"Carolyn, I know you are mad at me right now and I'm not even sure what you thought you saw but..."

I could barely hold back my anger as I growled into the phone.

"What I *thought* I saw? You mean what I *did* see! I saw everything. I am not stupid Christy! You should know that about me!"

My heart was racing in a rage. I was too smart not to see the manipulation, the plan, the truth. I let her have it.

"You were supposed to be my friend! My *best* friend!" I wanted to hang up.

"Carolyn, I still am. It was my fault. Your Dad doesn't think you saw anything and I told him you did but he still thinks you didn't because you didn't say anything."

"I saw your hand on his leg and his hand on your leg! I saw your hand in his crotch and his hand in your crotch! Did I miss anything?" My voice was shaking with hatred.

"I am so sorry, Carolyn. It's my fault. I started it. Ed is a good man."

"Why did he really drop me off first? Did you do it? Did he drop you off last so you could do it in the car?" I asked the questions not wanting answers.

"No, we just talked...that's all. He told me there was nothing between us. There's nothing between us Carolyn okay? Can I still be your friend?"

Christy's voice had changed to sadness.

"I need some time. I don't know what to think. I'm tired."

As I hung up the phone I knew I would forgive her. I also knew that I was forgiving her for the lie she had given me. It was easy to forgive something that wasn't true... much easier than demanding the truth.

* * * * *

I didn't see my father all week. Whether it was because he was avoiding me or because our schedules were just not the same, I would never know. In the mornings he was already gone by the time I was showered and made my way into the kitchen for a cup of coffee. Now that I was in high school I had taken on the habit of drinking black coffee for breakfast instead of eating cereal. I poured coffee from the percolator and could feel that it was only half full. Yep, Dad had come and gone. He was working late each night so it wasn't until Saturday afternoon that I saw him for the first time since the car ride incident. He came up and elbowed me.

"Hey Chump!" he said.

He was goofing around and I knew that nothing would be said. Either he really did think that I hadn't seen anything or he was making it clear that it would never be discussed. I always obeyed my father and I wished I hadn't seen what I did so I responded back.

"Hey Dad!" I said and gave him a hug.

Over the next month I slowly started talking to Christy again. We never spoke of the incident and it was easy to let it go. We started hanging out with other friends and I didn't try to persuade her to go to church anymore.

Basketball season was ending and it wouldn't be long before Track would be in full swing. I made an effort to complete all my homework so I could focus on the final basketball game. I hadn't been to very many games and felt bad that I hadn't been there to cheer Skip on. When I arrived I was surprised to see Ginger and Ragan hanging out. Ginger was a good friend of mine but Ragan and I didn't see eye to eye. Just as I entered the gym they whispered to each other and ran to the hall and into the girl's bathroom. I turned my attention back to the court just as Skip went in for a layup. He missed and swore under his breath. I waited until he redeemed himself with another lay up before waving. He smiled as he headed back down the court.

Try as they might, the Mighty Oilers could not get ahead in points. I stretched and headed to the restroom to freshen up. Right as I opened the door Ginger and Ragan looked up at me then hurried passed with a quick, "Hi. Bye." It was such strange behavior that I wondered if they had been doing drugs. I went into the stall and sat on the toilet to pee when I noticed a folded up square of notebook paper. It was obviously a note and as I picked it up I recognized the writing as Ginger's and the person it was addressed to read *Skip*.

My heart jumped into my throat. Not for one second did I consider giving it back to Ginger. I carefully unwrapped the perfume soaked paper and watched it blossom into fragments of big round letters. I knew her writing. We had passed notes back and forth for months in class. The letter was long and took up the full page. At the top was Skip's name with hearts on each side. I read about how she was in love with him, how hot she thought his body was and how she enjoyed being with him the other night. I read about how she was worried about me finding out and she was really worried about me beating her up. She wrote about how Ragan could protect her and fight me. Then I read about their plans for the weekend nights. Slowly I folded the letter back up as anger and then sadness filled my heart.

I knew that Ginger would put out for Skip if she hadn't already. She was a petite blonde with exaggerated curves and the boys couldn't help but watch her every move. She lived across the street from my house and I had seen boys going in and out of her house. I contemplated what I should do about the note. It was clear that Skip had cheated on me and clear that my friendship with Ginger wasn't strong enough for her to avoid my boyfriend. I walked out of the restroom and turned down the hall to head home when I saw Ginger and Ragan heading back toward me. They must have realized that they had dropped the note. Just as they started to pass I looked Ginger straight in the eyes.

"Ginger, you dropped something."
I handed her the note and blankly added, "You can have him."

Ginger froze in place as Ragan's mouth dropped in shock. I didn't say another word and slowly continued down the hall without looking back. I could hear Skip calling to me and Ginger quickly telling him to be quiet. The game was over and we had lost.

As I walked the eight blocks home I wondered if I should have let Skip go to second base with me. Would that have saved our relationship? I doubted it. There really wasn't a second base that I could tell. People usually went right from French kissing to doing it and everyone at school knew which girls were doing it. I wasn't ready to be known for that at school. Most importantly, I wasn't ready for my Dad to find out…or God. I wasn't sure which one I was more afraid of disappointing.

I wished that I could talk to Vernon about everything but he was happily going out with someone now. He would have listened but it would have been awkward. I didn't want to talk to anyone else about it, especially not Christy. When I got home I noticed that Donna was up in her room but the stairs were ominous, the emotional drain I felt was too much for stairs. Once I was in my room I belly-flopped onto my bed with a huge sigh and then slowly army crawled to the edge where I could reach my phone.

"Hello?" Donna's voice was the only one I wanted to hear. She was the only one I could ever trust.

* * * * *

As the weeks passed it was clear Skip and Ginger weren't meant for each other but by then I had moved on and was enjoying the art of flirting. Winter had passed but Spring was not about to let us off easy with a sweet, soft entrance. Snow had arrived once more. It wasn't the dry frilly snow but a mean icy snow that was much more difficult to walk in or drive on. I reached back in my closet for my boots one more time and met Donna at the door for our walk to school. As we opened the front door we could hear a strange spinning noise. We looked down the street and started snickering when we saw a blue Camaro Z28 sideways in the road. Lloyd was a Senior and loved his car so much that he had to drive it the 4 blocks to school every day.

His car wasn't going anywhere on this icy morning and his low profile tires were spinning 100 miles per hour. Donna and I smiled as we walked by his car, which hadn't moved an inch in the 4 blocks we had walked to reach him. As he grimaced I could see his metal front tooth. Lloyd was big from lifting weights and I couldn't imagine getting him mad. Quickly, I changed my smile to a sympathetic sorry and quickly turned down the street. If was strangely comforting to know that someone as tough as Lloyd was as vulnerable to the elements as the rest of us.

I started noticing Lloyd a lot more in the halls and when I went into the weight room he offered to spot me during squats. I had naturally strong legs and broad shoulders so I was able to lift a lot more than anyone expected. Slowly, the perception I had of Lloyd melted away and I realized he wasn't so tough and scary.

My confidence grew along with each squat and each flirt until I was sure that he was interested in me.

Lloyd was the only boy brave enough to come to my house. Whenever there was a knock at the door after school I would just continue with my homework while Donna raced to see which of her friends had arrived. But this time when she opened the door I heard her gasp so I went over to see what the trouble was. There was Lloyd standing in my doorway. His big burly body dwarfed Donna so that she looked like a little doll. Donna's eyes were wide as she stood frozen in place and I quickly became embarrassed. As I welcomed Lloyd into our home, I stepped over to Donna and punched her on the arm to release her from her stupor.

"That didn't hurt at all," she informed.

Just as I was ready to hit her again Lloyd spoke up.

"Oh, ya? You're pretty tough but I bet you can't win at bloody knuckles."

We both looked at him, intrigued. Donna and I considered ourselves pretty tough and there was nothing like a challenge to get our attention.

Once Lloyd explained the game it was pretty obvious that Donna would lose. Each one would take turns hitting the other's knuckles with their own knuckles until someone gave up by calling Uncle. As Lloyd removed his gaudy gold nugget ring and his class ring, I told Donna I thought this was a bad idea. She set her jaw in determination and placed her hands out in fists, waiting for the first hit.

"No," Lloyd said as he turned her fist sideways, "We do it this way and only with one hand today. Are you right handed?"

Donna nodded her head as she was clearly awestruck by a Senior holding her hand.

"Okay," Lloyd continued, "then we will do it with your left hand so you can still write."

I opened my mouth to protest but he quickly added, "I will stop as soon as you say Uncle."

It was up to Donna to decide when she had enough so I figured after one or two hits she would give up and I could actually spend some time with Lloyd myself. That was until Donna spoke.

"Or when you give up."

The look in Donna's eyes was no longer infatuation; it was pure determination and stubbornness. Lloyd told her to go first so she raised her closed fist high in the air, inhaled deeply and dropped it as fast as she could…and missed. Lloyd laughed as her face turned red.

"That was your first time so I'm going to give you another chance but if you miss again your turn is over. I suggest you don't go so high so you can control your aim a little better."

Again, Donna raised her fist high in the air then, remembering the expert advice, lowered it half way. Her fist hit its target and Donna howled as she grabbed her hand. Lloyd was like stone, not a single flinch. He gave her his metal tooth smile.

"Now, it's my turn."

I wanted to stop the game but Donna said, "Bring it on, Buddy Boy!"

Lloyd only lifted his fist half a foot above her hand and came down with a *whack!* right on the edge of her knuckles. Donna growled this time instead of yelling and I knew it hurt. Her knuckles were red. This went on for a good ten minutes before I called the game. I had hoped that Lloyd would stop on his own after realizing that Donna would never ever call Uncle even if every knuckle was cracked open. Donna's knuckles were huge, red and swollen. I told her we would need to ice them to get the swelling down and silently hoped that Dad and Cindy wouldn't notice. Lloyd's knuckles were red and I could tell that Donna was more than he had bargained.

"C'mon I'll show ya my house," I called to him after filling a baggy with ice.

Lloyd didn't seem too impressed with the house until we got to my bedroom. He laughed at the colors and said how he wouldn't have expected me to be an orange and yellow type person. I quickly explained that I was young when I picked the colors and that I was definitely a blue type person now. I went to my window and quickly closed the window and the curtains. Anyone that walked up to the door could see right into my room. I had to make sure there was time to sneak Lloyd out the back door if my Dad showed up. When I turned around, Lloyd was laying on my bed smiling.

"What are you doing lying on my bed?" My cheeks blushed.

"It's nice. Come try it out." He patted the bed and turned on his side.

"I don't want to."

"Awww, are you afraid of me?"

"Not at all."

Slowly I started to lie next to him when he grabbed me by the waist and pulled me to his chest. His chest was enormous and solid. Just as I started to wrestle away he placed his hand behind my head and with a gentle yet determined pressure brought my head down to his face.

"I'm going to kiss you now okay?"

I was breathless so I could only nod. Before I could regain my composure his tongue was in my mouth, his lips pressing my own lips against my teeth until they felt swollen and chapped. As I focused on keeping my teeth from pinching my upper lip I heard a zipper and realized Lloyd had unzipped my jeans and was quickly making his way to my underwear. I grabbed his hand.

"No!" I said.

He stopped immediately and looked at me, "Okay, okay. I'm not going to do anything you don't want to do. We'll just kiss, that's nice right?"

I nodded as I zipped my jeans back up.

As we continued kissing he kept his hands over my clothes and I felt the desire to move my hands over his chest. Once I put my hand up his shirt I felt his kiss become stronger and more passionate. Afraid he might try my zipper again I started to pull my hand back when he grabbed it and placed it on his jeans right over his own zipper, then moved my hand back and forth. I could feel his penis getting hard and wondered if the jeans could hold it back. Intrigued by these changes to his body I continued to rub and went from the back and forth motion to a circular one. Suddenly, he was rock hard and I sensed the urgency in his kiss. With his left hand he unbuttoned and unzipped his jeans then quickly grabbed my hand, placing it directly on his penis. Then, without letting go of my hand, he started moving our hands up and down. This was all way too new for me and I pulled away.

"Please, Carolyn." He pleaded. "Haven't you ever touched one?"

My fear was stronger than the embarrassment.

"No, I haven't and I can't yet. I'm sorry."

I was sorry and it was clear how vulnerable he was. Slowly he got up and went to my bathroom. When he came back out he told me I was a good girl and left. I sat back down on my bed and thought about how his body had made me feel. I was so tempted to please him. It would have been easy to keep going...maybe all the way and it was really hard to focus, let alone to make him stop doing something that felt so good. I wondered if Christy had wanted to stop when Lloyd was with her but was too weak to resist. Lloyd knew I was a virgin just as I knew he had been with Christy. I wondered if Lloyd would have stopped if my Dad hadn't been a cop.

* * * * *

I turned 15 years old in May without any excitement or party. The most exciting thing that I had going on was track. I was doing well in track and especially well at the high jump. The only problem was that I approached the jump like a left-handed person which meant that as all the competitors lined up on the right side to circle around to the bar I was over on the left waiting for my turn. A lot of times the officials didn't notice me and I'd miss a turn, then I would have to jump twice in a row.

Church was becoming a chore due to my deep desire to sleep in on Sundays. Donna and Cindy were arguing more often. One day, Cindy came completely unglued when she discovered a half eaten piece of cake under Donna's bed. Donna yelled back for the first time and Cindy didn't know what to do. I was just surprised that it had taken so long to happen. Dad was making little remarks about Cindy, here and there, about her looks and weight. I giggled when he made the comments but it was only for his sake. It upset me that he was criticizing her and I wasn't sure what to make of it.

I was happy when I could get out of the house and was going to stay the night with Amy for a change. When I went to her house no one barreled down the stairs like they had the first time I stayed the night with Christy. They were all still up upstairs but the tape on the floor had been removed. Amy had moved into the cubby area by the window with Christy so the three of us just sat and talked a lot about nothing. Finally, Amy looked at Christy and said, "Hand it over."

Christy gave her a *not in front of Carolyn* look that was too obvious not to be noticed.
"I don't care, give it to me," Amy insisted.

Christy was older but Amy was more determined and could raise problems if she wanted so Christy lifted her blanket and handed Amy a bottle that contained dark amber liquid. Amy took a small swig and handed it to me. It was Jack Daniels whiskey. I had never had whiskey! Just as Christy was about to protest, I lifted the bottle to my mouth and chugged. The molten lava coursed down my throat, surely removing the lining of my esophagus as it went. I coughed as the liquor coated my stomach with fire. Amy laughed, smacking my back in some sort of ritual to get me to stop coughing as Christy grabbed the bottle.

"You can't drink it like that. That's too much. Now you will get sick." Christy said.

Amy rolled her eyes, "No, she won't mommy. She'll be fine."

I looked at Christy squarely and as new courage raced through my blood I made sure to accentuate every word so there would be no question as to their meaning.

"I...will...be...fine."

Christy knew there was an unspoken understanding between us now so she remained silent as I grabbed the bottle from her grip, happily took another swig and decided, "I am in love with Jack Daniels!" Christy laughed with me while Amy offered me a puff off her cigarette. I was about to decline and then thought, well why the hell not?

It wasn't long until I felt the full affects of the whiskey. I felt too tired to talk anymore so I curled up between Christy and Amy's mattresses and fell asleep to the humming sounds of sisters reminiscing about other times.

* * * * *

My freshman year came to an end with a sense of sadness for the loss of innocence. Not the loss of sexual innocence. I was definitely still a virgin. But the innocence of a daughter who thinks her father is perfect and that a friend has no secrets, the belief that a boyfriend is always loyal and that going to church automatically made things better.

I could sense the storm racing toward me, stirring up doubt and clouding my faith.

Chapter 7

Wind

I love you,
I love you not.

I love your summer whisper
Upon my skin,
Dreaming of cool days
Yet to begin.

I love not your winter grasp
Upon my back
Or vicious power to make
Trees snap.

I love your fresh perfume
Clearing away
The smothering dullness of a
hot day.

I love not your willingness to
Fling cold rain
In my face and eyes, making me
Go insane.

I love your nurturing spirit
Answering needs
By dancing through the plains
Scattering seeds.

I love you,
I love you not.

Carolyn A. Ames

Just as the wind is able to go from a twisted, menacing tornado to a carefree breeze playing amongst the oaks, so goes life.

My relationship with Ragan had taken such a turn of fate. She had decided that Ginger wasn't such a great friend to have and grew tired of her. Slowly, she started talking to me about things and we started to grow closer. She lived across from the Mondle boys and I figured that if Vernon and his brothers thought she was okay then she must be.

Ragan was hard for me to figure out at first. During the fall of our freshman year she appeared to resent me and rumors circled around school that she wanted to beat me up. During volleyball practice one Friday we were the last two in a competition of endurance. Our coach had everyone place their backs against the wall and then slide down the wall into a sitting position, as if we were sitting in an actual chair. The rest was simple, stay in that position as long as possible. Slowly, each team member fell to the floor but Ragan and I remained. I looked over at her, recognizing the determination in her face. If I were to win this competition my determination had to be stronger.

As time went on, our legs started to shake in uncontrolled spasms. Ragan groaned and flipped her straight brown bangs out of her freckled face. Her skin was a golden tan which made her thighs even more defined and her muscles bulged with the evidence of all our hard practices. She placed her hands on her thighs to silence the spasms but the coach quickly reminded us of the "no hands" rule. Ragan glanced my way but I showed no sign that I was ready to give up. My legs were in full spasms as I leaned my head back and closed my eyes. I would not give up to her no matter what the cost. Suddenly I heard Ragan collapse to the mat in tears as our team mates ran over to console her. As I slid the rest of the way down to the mat I could see her place both hands to her face and shoo the team away. I swallowed hard. She wasn't crying because she lost, she was crying because she was able to push herself to the limit and then go just beyond that limit. I felt the same emotion she did but before I could say anything she gave me a dirty look and limped off.

Things came to a head during an away game. As I was exiting the bus Ragan quietly mumbled "Bitch." I had had enough and quickly turned around to face her. She stood in the aisle of the bus as I unleashed my frustration.

"I have done nothing to you! You call me a bitch and you don't even know me! You want to fight? Then let's get off this bus and fight right now. I am sick of this! Why do you hate me so much?"

I could feel my body start to shake. I didn't want to fight but I didn't know what else to do. This had to end one way or another. If it meant that she beat me up then so be it.

Ragan opened her mouth but nothing came out for a few seconds.

Finally, she stammered, "I don't hate you. I thought you hated me!"

Then it was my turn to be shocked. She thought I hated *her*?

Very matter-of-factly I stated, "Well, I don't hate you. I don't even know you."

"Well, then I'm not going to fight you."

"I'm not going to fight you either."

I started to ask her if she wanted to talk later but one of the senior players yelled at us to get off the bus. Not wanting to get in a fight with a senior, I quickly did as I was told and headed to the locker room to get ready for the game.

Even though we no longer hated each other, we didn't become friends until after the Ginger and Skip episode. Ragan smoked cigarettes and swore like a sailor. I was shocked at the string of cuss words she could put together without repeating a single one. She didn't think piss was a swear word at all and I admired her ability to place it in every sentence. Ragan's parents were divorced and I discovered that she had one in Washington just like we did. She had lived in Midwest since elementary school but she was a transplant just like I was. It didn't matter how long you lived in these towns, if you weren't born there then you were always considered an outsider. It wasn't a bad feeling. I just figured that so many families came and went that it must be easier not to fully accept an outsider than to accept them only to have to tell them good-bye. Besides, there were enough outsiders to befriend, to more than make up for the inability to fully penetrate the inner circle and I wasn't convinced that it would be worth the effort.

Summer was beginning and it was finally time to make our road trip to Washington. Ragan and Christy were traveling with us this time so Donna and I were really excited. Ragan was going to visit her Dad in Seattle and Christy came along to spend a couple weeks with us at our Mom's home. We loved the road trip and the adventures of traveling. Ragan would be fun. She had a giggle that softened her sharp tongue and a great sense of humor.

The trip from Wyoming to Washington could be done within 24 hours but we were taking a longer route and preferred to have shorter driving days. We stayed the first night in a hotel that had a huge swimming pool with slides, an arcade and pool tables. Dad set us up in our own room and he took the one next door. Our room was huge but we were more excited about having time to hang out in the pool area. There were a lot of people and the promise of good-looking guys seemed a sure thing. Quickly, we changed into our swimsuits...that is...all except Christy. She wasn't feeling well and wanted to lie down for awhile. It seemed to me like she had been feeling just fine but I knew that she didn't really enjoy swimming around as much as we did and figured it was a good excuse. I didn't' want her to do anything she didn't enjoy so I told her I would check back later to see how she was doing.

We were only gone from the room for twenty minutes before Ragan decided she needed a smoke. As she ran to the room Donna and I toweled off.

"I'm hungry," Donna announced, "swimming always makes me hungry."

I told her that I was pretty sure we had some chips left over in the room and we could check to see when we could go to dinner. When we got to the room, Ragan was sitting at the table smoking one of Christy's cigarettes. Dad didn't know she smoked so she bummed them from Christy.

"Where's Christy?" I asked as I scanned the room.

"Dunno," Ragan answered, "the fucking room was empty when I got here but at least the smokes were here. I was going to have a shit fit if they were gone."

That didn't even make sense to me so I didn't respond, but instead said, "I'm going to go ask Dad when we can eat dinner. We're hungry. I bet Christy went to find us at the pool. I don't know how she missed us."

I threw Donna the bag of chips and walked out the door. Dad's room was to the right so I only had to take two steps. Just as I started to knock I could hear him talking to someone. He must be on the phone with Cindy letting her know what hotel we were staying in. I knocked a tune and waited. No answer. It was silent. He must have hung up the phone. I knocked again.

"Dad? It's Carolyn. We want to know when we can go eat."

After a short silence Dad opened the door. The room was smoky and I squinted my eyes. Christy was sitting on the edge of the bed with a cigarette.

"Oh," I was surprised, "I was wondering where you were."

"I went to look for you," she responded, "but didn't see you anywhere so I came to ask Ed if he knew."

"Were you feeling better and wanting to go swimming?"
"Ya, I'm feelin' better now."

I knew she was lying. She didn't have her suit on.
"Well, maybe after we eat then," I added and turned to leave.

Whatever was going on, I didn't want to know. It was obvious no one was going to tell me anyway.

* * * * *

We got a late start the next morning. Usually, Dad was an early riser but he seemed tired and had slept well past 9am. The hotel had a continental breakfast but we were too late so we decided to make some time on the road before stopping for lunch. It was already warm outside and any trace of morning dew had evaporated. The flies were already buzzing about but luckily for us they weren't horse flies and didn't bite. Ragan and I sat in the front so I took on the role of navigator and grabbed the atlas from the dash to make sure my Dad was going in the right direction. I knew it wasn't necessary since he had travelled this land many times but it was fun to think I might catch him getting lost. I loved looking at maps. Rather than heading north to Interstate 90 through Montana like we had the last time, we journeyed south to Interstate 80 and skirted across the top portion of Utah. We would be travelling on the east side of The Great Salt Lake which showed up on the map in blue and it was definitely huge. I glanced down on the map and noticed the Grand Canyon. That would have been fun to see again. This route didn't seem to have a lot of exciting landmarks along the way but that didn't really matter since we had company.

The terrain had changed from the drab beige prairie to a contrast of orange-red dirt, dark green trees and a deep blue sky with white cotton ball clouds. Utah was shockingly beautiful with colors of the rainbow spilled out all over the land. Purple and magenta waves sleepily winded their way amongst the cliffs while green ponderosa pine and varieties of spruce dotted the hillsides. I wondered why this land was not more populated but then reminded myself how deceiving the plains could be and that I was not going to assume, like so many tourists, that what I see is all there is. Surely, there were cattle ranches and fish-filled streams beyond the highway.

As we passed through Ogden Dad started telling us about the Mormons and polygamy. We listened intently as he spoke of men that had more than one wife and huge families. It was common for the women to be very young, even our ages, when married. I tried to imagine myself married at 15 years old. It didn't' seem to far-fetched actually since I already could do all of the household chores and could cook and sew. Dad talked about how girls were married as young as 14. When a girl could bear children she could get married. I wasn't so sure about that since I was 11 years old when I started my period and the thought of giving birth at that age was crazy. I looked over at Ragan and saw that her face was all scrunched up in disgust. Obviously she didn't like the idea at all. Christy, on the other hand, had straightened up her back and was appearing more womanly by the moment. She was, after all, 16 years old and according to what Dad was telling us, was practically an old maid in Bible times.

We left Utah and said hello to Idaho. Well, Donna said hello to Idaho about 20 times, enjoying the rhyme while we all rolled our eyes. Idaho didn't strike me as too exciting. The colors of the land were leaning toward the beige I was used to in Wyoming. As we crossed through the Snake River Plain I noticed large dust devils on the horizon. We had all gone quiet in the afternoon heat and all the windows were rolled down in the Chrysler. I watched intently as my favorite river came into view. Its rocks were rounded and the water ran clear. The Snake was an inviting river and birds seemed attracted to it. I imagined myself wandering its banks until I discovered a deep pool to jump into and cool down. It had hiding spots that would be perfect for fishing and many twists and turns for tubing. It was the perfect river and I thought that someday I might live by the Snake.

We were heading west as the sun set so our faces were all aglow and my eyes squinted to see ahead. Dad had big cop sunglasses on and Ragan was wearing black mirrored sunglasses that made her look like a rocker chick. My sunglasses were in my bag in the trunk so I had to put my hand above my eyes to shade them. I felt like I was saluting to the world. Finally, we stopped for dinner and the night. We were all tired and quiet compared to the night before.

Once I settled into the lumpy motel bed and Christy turned out the lights, I thought about Mom. She was probably running around like a chicken with her head cut off trying to get the house ready. I smiled at the thought and could feel my stomach leap as I realized I would be there within 24 hours. I missed her so much and couldn't wait to hug her. The first couple of weeks were always a big transition for me and I tended to act like a jerk. It was hard to switch gears between staying with my Dad and staying with my Mom. They were two different worlds and it was hard for me not to compare them. I hoped that this time I would adjust better and that maybe having Christy and Ragan there for a few days would help with that. I turned over my lumpy motel pillow to feel the cool side and meant to remind Donna that we would be in Washington soon but fell asleep before I could utter a word.

* * * * *

Dad woke us up early by calling our motel phone. The red light flashed as the tinny ring blared in my ear drums. I jumped up and raced to answer it before could ring again. Dad was headed for the motel's restaurant for coffee and wanted us to meet him there. When I hung up the phone I was surprised to see that no one was awake. My ears were still ringing from the phone but Donna was completely out with her body vicariously balanced on the edge of the bed. Ragan was sprawled across it diagonally with the covers wadded up at her side. I looked back at my bed and Christy was lying completely straight with her hands folded at her stomach like a corpse. Her mouth was wide open as if she were trying to catch popcorn out of the air. Just as I began to yell for them to get up I quickly changed my mind and headed for the shower. I was going to have hot water for a change.

After breakfast we were back on the road with renewed energy. The sky was still a light yellowish-blue from the morning sun and the air was clean with the start of a new day. Donna and Ragan were in the front this time. Donna coerced Ragan into playing "I Spy" so Ragan was searching everywhere for "something purplish, brownish". Christy didn't seem interested in riding up front and I thought it might be to prove some unspoken point which I was going to ignore anyway. In an effort to lighten things up between us I started talking about slugs. It worked. Christy was completely engrossed as I explained that slugs look like big snails without shells and are mostly water so when you pour salt on them they melt away into a big blob of slime. She thought I was just putting her on so I went on to tell her about the time I was playing in the backyard and stepped on a black one in my bare feet. The slug squished between my toes and the slim was sticky like pitch so by the time I made it to the water hose the dirt and slime wouldn't come off. I had to hop on one foot into the bathroom to use hot water and soap before I could get back to building my fort. She seemed content with my story after that and made me promise to find her a slug before she had to go back to Wyoming.

It was mid-afternoon when I noticed the trees. Instead of spots of trees scattered here and there they were becoming forests and growing taller by the minute. Christy gazed in awe at the Douglas Firs towering at the side of the road. Dad pulled over and we all got out of the car to stretch. Christy walked over to the tree, touching its bark and stared straight up at the cone laden branches.

"I have never seen a tree this big!" she exclaimed. "The bark is so thick."

"That one isn't that big," I happily proclaimed.

"Ya," Donna chimed in, "that ones nothin' like we have in our yard."

Christy was dumbfounded, "You have trees bigger than this in your own yard?!"

"Yup." Donna hugged the tree like it was an old friend. "I miss the trees."

"Welcome to Washington," I smiled.

Within an hour the trees devoured the landscape and the hills were drenched in shades of dark green. Christy had gone completely quiet as she stared out the window. I felt a sense of pride and longing that I couldn't quite understand. I spent a lot of times playing and thinking amongst the fir trees in my backyard. Growing up with 7 family members made for a crowded house so we spent a lot of time in the backyard. The ground was dirt because grass wouldn't grow in the shade. We ran around the yard bare foot unless we were playing hide and seek. We were serious about hide and seek. Once it was announced that we would be playing the game everyone would run into the house and search our clothes for the best camouflage we could find.

My step-brother, Tim, was my greatest competition. He was 6 years older than me, bigger, and faster. My only chance at winning would be to hide better. I had a special long-sleeved dark navy shirt that I wore with jeans no matter how hot it was. Skin color does not blend in with green salal or brown bark. Once everyone was dressed we would meet in the middle of our backyard and decide who would be "it" then the fun would begin. My technique for hiding was very simple. I loved the woods and became one with nature by simply running in a direction and literally diving into the undergrowth as if it were a swimming pool. Wherever I landed was my hiding spot. It didn't matter if I landed on fallen branches or a spider web; I was there to stay until the end. I had a chance to study nature up close and personal as I peeked between the broad leafed underbrush at little spiders, riley pole potato bugs, and centipedes. There was nothing poisonous to worry about so I could examine my backyard life to my heart's content, or until I was found by the seeker. If I were lucky I would land softly on a bouquet of ferns next to a wild huckleberry bush so I could snack on the tart little berries while watching Donna tackle Terry and announce that she had been found.

The only flaw to my hiding strategy was discovered when Tim had used a similar technique – only he didn't dive into the brush, he ran upright through the underbrush and behind a tree. Within a matter of seconds he let out a howl and came running toward the house with his hands waving in the air. The way he was yelling and seeing his orange hair flying all over the place as he bolted out of the woods made me want to laugh…until I realized what had happened. He had stepped right onto a wasp's nest and was being stung over and over again. After that I considered changing my technique but then came to the conclusion that his mistake had been in hiding across the cul-de-sac in the neighboring trees instead of in our backyard. I knew our yard and would know if there was a wasp's nest being erected.

I doubted that Christy and Ragan would want to play hide and seek. We were much too mature for that now and besides, they would be too easy to find since they wouldn't realize the bugs, frogs and garter snakes were harmless. They were used to rattlers and black widows.

About an hour outside of my home town we saw a sign for Mount St. Helen's that had a closed sign plastered across the middle of it. The mud and trees from the landslide still suffocated the Toutle River as we crossed over it. I would never forget the day she erupted. We had all climbed on top of our neighbor's roof and watched as the dark gray mushroom cloud boiled up miles into the sky. We sat there wondering how long it would take for the ash and lava to kill us. We had been reassured that the lava would never make it to our house but when the ash started falling from the sky we were told to stay inside because the ash was like glass to our lungs.

We exited the Interstate in Tumwater and I started pointing out landmarks to Christy and Ragan. My favorite mountain, Mount Rainier was to the east of us. As we drove west around Black Lake I explained that the hydroplanes would be racing on the lake in July so we wouldn't be able to swim in it after that because they bring up all the muck from the bottom of the lake. I told the story about the mythical Black Lake turtle that was the size of a bus and lived at the bottom. It was exciting to see the lake, knowing it would only be minutes now until I saw my Mom.

Everyone was getting fidgety in the car as Dad drove into the housing development. "We're here!" Donna yelled as we made our way into the cul-de-sac. Our green house came into view and I instinctively reached for the car door. I wanted to jump out before the car was even parked. "I see Tara!" Donna yelled again. Sure enough, I could see Tara standing in front of the big picture window of the living room. She was jumping up and down and pointing. Her thick straight brown hair was swinging from side to side. All of a sudden I saw another person walk over to Tara, peer out the window and then rush to the front door...it was Mom.

* * * * *

The time with our friends went fast and before we knew it Ragan was up North with her Dad and Christy was flying back home to her family. Mom and Leroy made them feel very welcome in our home. We had a huge barbeque and invited extended family so the place was packed with fun-loving people. There was a watermelon eating contest that Donna won thanks to her strategy of eating everything as fast as possible and blowing it out her nose. We taught Ragan and Christy how to walk on our home-made stilts that were constructed of one long small tree from the backyard with its limbs and bark peeled off and one chunk of 2x4 nailed haphazard to the little tree to form a platform.

We had gotten so good on the stilts that we could walk and dance on them all day without touching the ground. We went on walks to the neighborhood store so Christy and Ragan could buy smokes and then down to the lake to sunbathe on the dock. We even found a long green slug for Christy to salt but she refused. She liked the slug too much to kill it and it took some convincing to make her realize she couldn't take it on the plane back to Wyoming with her.

As the early August summer heat slowed everything down, I spent most of my afternoons walking to the store and lake or laying in our front yard drinking tea and tanning. It gave me a lot of time to think and my mind drifted off to the past year and everything that had happened. What was really going on with Christy and my Dad? Was this some childish infatuation that had gone too far? I thought about how many young women had been around us during the years. We had babysitters for two of the summers that we stayed with Dad that were equally as "infatuated" with him. One had actually threatened us by saying she could have Dad marry her any time she wanted. It was a normal thing for girls to have a crush on someone that was an officer of the law, guitar player, singer, teacher, paramedic, and hunter and on and on. He was smart and very good looking for an old man in his thirties. His blue eyes were hypnotic and girls would just stare and smile. But as easy as it was to accept these girls having crushes on my father, my stomach turned over whenever I would think about how Christy was when she was around him and the dark night in the car would come to the front of my mind again and I would remember what I saw. That sick stomach feeling made me angry and I decided to walk it out by going to the store. I had on my favorite cut off jeans that rode high with dangly white strings hanging amongst my thighs and I knotted my plaid button up shirt just like Daisy Duke from the Dukes of Hazard. I slipped my thongs between my toes and headed down the hill by myself. I knew there was no way to run away from the feeling I had but I didn't know how to deal with it either. I was annoyed that I should even have to deal with it at all.

Frustration and anger made me feel vulnerable so in an effort to be tough and daring I decided to buy a pack of smokes. I was immediately excited about this sinful idea and wondered if I could actually pull it off. The only way it could work was if I walked into the store like I owned it and had bought cigarettes a million times before. I'd need to seem bored...bored with all the cigarette buying because I buy so many packs every day.

I pushed open the glass door and right away the store clerk said hello. I smiled a bored half smile and immediately turned left toward the Pepsi. I sauntered over to the pop section and sighed a deep "I'm so bored" sigh and grabbed one of the 16 ounce glass bottles. The faster my heart beat the slower I walked, reminding myself that I was cool and could do this. Ragan could do it so why couldn't I do it?

Once at the counter I could hear myself say, as if on autopilot, "Pack of smokes please." I did it!

Just as I began to feel too cool for my own good the store clerk asked, "What brand?"

Well, I hadn't thought about that. My Mom smoked Salem menthols, Dad smoked Winstons and Christy and Ragan smoked Marlboro so I answered, "Marlboro reds, hard pack."

As the clerk turned to get my cigarettes I felt a twinge of sadness and I knew that if that clerk would turn around and tell me I was too young to smoke that I would leave and never try it again. But instead he threw down the Marlboros with a free pack of matches and I paid the $1.10.

On the way back home I smoked my first cigarette by myself. It wasn't at all enjoyable but I was determined to be a smoker so I hid the hard pack in the front of my shorts between the zipper and my belly which instantly made me feel sexy. This would be the second secret that I was keeping from Donna.

Summer came to an abrupt end and as we drove the 90 minutes to Sea-Tac Airport I realized that I wasn't nearly as excited to go back to Wyoming as usual but I was sure it was the best thing to do. I was anxious to see Ragan and to smoke with her. I might even swear now and then while I smoked just to show her how tough I had become. I was going to be a sophomore and I knew that the year would be much different from my freshman year. I was stronger and more daring with secrets. I glanced over at Donna and recognized the sober silence as she had already began to miss Mom...the transition from Washington to Wyoming had started.

Chapter 8

Blind Faith

The start of my sophomore year was anticlimactic and would have been boring except for the fact that there were a few new faces in the school for everyone to fall in love with for awhile. Cindy had made us a few shirts but there was no big trip to go clothes shopping. That was fine with me since my clothes were comfortable and broken in. Donna was taking longer than usual to transition but once she spent some quality time with Mandy the sadness melted away and she was laughing again.

Volleyball practice was harder than ever with a new coach that obviously knew what she was doing. She was short with very short blonde hair to match and was a strong athlete so we couldn't get away with anything. Right from the beginning she had us diving and jumping, crouching and spiking all over the gym floor. The highlight of practice was watching the football players walk by on their way down to the field. I was free to look at them all and, being the new daring person that I was, I gave a couple of the boys an extra long look, which startled one and embarrassed another. Ragan smiled and a few of the girls seemed confused at my new assertiveness which made me even happier.

We had an Indian summer which stretched into late September and the dry dusty ground cracked in despair. The infrequent thunderstorms brought little, if any, rain. I cherished the warm fall wind that carried the dying leaves to their final resting place. There was a great sense of change all about. It was in the wind, in my home and in my soul. Dad and Cindy seemed miles away as we trudged through each day...get up...go to work...come home...have dinner...clean up...go to bed...get up... Something was different but I couldn't get past my own changes to figure it out.

On Sunday evening all four of us went to church together, which had become pretty rare. Usually, Dad was out on patrol or would meet us there. But on this night Dad had a little talk with Donna and me prior to the evening worship. He said that Rev. Dewey was going to pray for us. Donna and I looked at each other, each with a "not again" look on our faces.

"Some people are saying things about me." Dad explained. "These people are starting rumors and accusing me of doing things so Rev. Dewey is going to bring it up to the congregation for prayer."

"What kinda things, Dad?" Donna asked.

"It doesn't matter what things. They aren't true but they are making it hard on Christy."

Dad glanced at me and then went on, "Christy's parents are trying to make me look bad but they don't have anything against me. Folks that have been in trouble with the law think that's a good idea and are trying to start trouble."

Donna and I both nodded that we understood. I understood a little too much and my mouth went dry.

It was stuffy sitting in the pew and I wanted to run out into the night, to free myself. I felt anxious, afraid that Christy's parents might show up at the church. I wondered where Christy was and if she knew what was going on. I wondered if Christy had told her parents about that night in the car. I wondered what the church people would do if they found out the truth.

Rev. Dewey began his sermon. I wished he would just hurry up and get to the part about Dad so it would be over. I didn't want the attention of being prayed for and wished we could just go home. We were the ones normally praying for others that were sick or were having hard times.

Our pastor began with the well known lessons of "judge not lest ye be judged" and "do unto others as you would have them do unto you" and then paused at length as he looked at the ceiling, his hands clasped together at his stomach. Slowly he swayed back and forth as he studied us, his face more serious than I had ever seen it.

Then he began, "Brothers...sisters...tonight one of our very own brothers is being persecuted by lies against him. He came to me and asked for my help. Some town folks are saying that he has done things, accusing him of sins he did not commit...in an effort to destroy his character." He paused again.

The church was still, quiet in anticipation of details. Rev. Dewey glanced at my father and my father nodded in approval so he went on.

"Brother Ed has done great things for this community..."

Everyone tried not to look over at us but it was too tempting. Their heads faced forward but their eyes strained our way.

"...he has saved lives, captured criminals and helped build a church with his own two hands. He is a child of God. The Bible tells of God's children being persecuted and we see this happening even in our small town."

Several people began to nod in agreement and I heard an "Amen".

Rev. Dewey moved closer to the edge of the stage, paused again and then confessed, "After Brother Ed left my home, after he told me his story, I got down on my knees..." The pastor began to cry a little and my heart pounded. I had no idea this was going to be so serious.

"...and I prayed to God Almighty not to let Satan plant the seed of doubt in my heart. I asked the Good Lord to speak to me and give me Truth and Light so that I may do the right thing by my church and my brothers and sisters."

Slowly, Rev. Dewey began to smile as if he were seeing something magnificent.

"Well, brothers and sisters, the Lord did speak to me and I know that Brother Ed is innocent of these accusations against him and we must pray for him to be strong and have faith that the Lord God Almighty will deliver him from this persecution."

I could hear more Amen's and Hallelujahs as my stomach tightened and the first lightning bolt pierced my heart.

I could barely breathe as our pastor led everyone in prayer. My mind raced as I thought about what I had just heard. God spoke to our pastor and said Dad was innocent yet I knew he wasn't...I saw with my own eyes what had happened in the car. I saw the looks that Dad and Christy gave to each other and I witnessed visits that were shrouded in mystery. What should I do? I looked over at my father and Cindy as they bowed their heads obediently in prayer, their faces smooth and relaxed as if everything was going to be fine now that they were praying. Slowly, I looked over my shoulder at Fred, our version of a prophet and noticed a pained look on his face as he prayed with all his soul. Finally, I glanced over at Jenny, Cindy's best friend, and was greeted with open eyes. Quickly, I turned back and slammed my eyes shut. I prayed to God but it wasn't for my Dad. I prayed that the service would end and I could go home.

It was silent in the car during the drive home and few words were spoken at home. I was happy to go to my room and shut off the lights. Tossing and turning I replayed Rev. Dewey's speech in my mind as I looked up at my dark ceiling. Satan must have tricked Rev. Dewey. At least Fred should have felt the truth…someone in that church should have known. Maybe Jenny knew and that was why her eyes were open during the prayer. Why did this have to happen now? I had no one to talk to and it was clear that God wasn't talking either.

* * * * *

School on Monday had a way of erasing Sunday evening worship by the mere act of walking down the school halls. The energy of teenagers vibrated off the lockers and kicked my pulse up a notch. Before I knew it I had forgotten all about the prayer session and was fully engaged in Geometry. As Greg asked the teacher a question I thought about what it would be like to date him. He was growing taller and getting handsome like his older brother. It was obvious that he was in love with Lisa though. It would probably never work between us anyway. He would have high expectations and that would be exhausting. That was too bad since I really enjoyed listening to him talk about things. He was really smart.

During lunch I walked with a group of girls to the store for Chuckwagons and Ragan asked if I could stay at her house Friday. I knew the answer from Dad would be no but I told her I would ask anyway. When I approached my father about staying the night he initially said no and I didn't question him but then he later changed his mind for some unknown reason. It didn't matter what the reason was, I only wanted to think about me for a change.

Since Ragan's house was across from the post office I just walked the 8 blocks with my bag. Ragan's mother was working so we were free to do what we wanted. It was a warm evening with a clear sky so we decided to go walking around town. I felt independent of everything. It was as if I was on my own and isolated because no one knew what I knew and I couldn't tell anyone. Even with Ragan's friendship I didn't dare reveal my secret. It made me feel destructive and I was ready to take some chances.

As we walked up the street toward the high school we saw Amy at her boyfriend's house. Amy was excited to introduce us to Fran and offered us each a Michelob beer. I felt very mature holding my bottle of beer and decided I should have a cigarette to go with it. After visiting for awhile we accepted another beer and headed back toward Ragan's were we met up with Vernon and a couple of his friends. They were headed toward the water tower so we decided to join them.

The water tower was the type that sat high on four legs and had the town's name on it as if we wouldn't know whose water it was without it plastered in big letters. I had passed the water tower thousands of times but never really considered it as a destination. Vernon and his friend Brian began climbing the tower's ladder and my adrenaline raced with excitement. Vernon saw the look on my face and smiled down at me. "Come on up!" he chimed. I didn't need coaxing as I quickly made my way up behind him. The ladder was straight up and much higher than it appeared. I looked down and could see everyone looking up at us. After what seemed like forever I reached the last leg of the ladder which bent back at a dangerous angle. I considered going back down but Vernon and Brian were already on the platform that circled the tower.

Vernon could tell I was afraid and told me it was okay to go back down but that the view was amazing. I took another step and bent my toes downward to help me hang on. My arms were burning with exhaustion and I knew that I had to make it to the platform. Not because I was determined but because I was too tired to go back down without resting. I figured the two beers I drank must have made me a little weaker because I should have been able to make it without being this tired. Four more rungs and I would be there. Brian was already on the other side of the tower with his spray paint. Vernon put his hand out as I reached the platform. It was at an awkward angle that made me use my upper strength and I struggled to inch my stomach onto the platform.

Once I was able to rest a minute I took a look around. I could see everything – the school, the store, the park and the house where Amy's boyfriend lived. The platform had an outward slant that made me feel like I could slide off. As I looked down I gasped out loud to discover how high I really was. Our friends at the bottom were tiny and I felt shaky. How would I ever get down? As I walked around the tower my fear gave way to excitement as I gazed upon the small town. The blocks were amazingly square with little round blobs of green trees. Half way around I saw Brian making his mark but before I could read what he painted, yells from below caught my attention. We made our way back to the front and looked down.

The man and woman that lived next door were standing by the ladder. They were the parents of a boy Donna had a crush on.

"Who's up there?" the woman yelled.

Silence.

"Answer me or I will call the police. Who's up there?" she yelled again.

Encouraged that she didn't say she already called the police Brian and Vernon yelled down their names.

"Okay, who else is there? I see three of you."

For some reason I felt compelled to lie. It was a lame lie but I wanted to see if I could get away with it so I finally yelled down, "It's Donna."

"Donna?" she sounded surprised. "Donna, come down the ladder. It's dangerous up there and if you don't come down I will call your father."

Once I realized they were not going to call my Dad I was more than happy to come down. I stepped toward the ladder and then realized that it was going to be harder to go down than it was going up and one mistake meant I would be dead. I had to turn around and face the tower while putting my stomach on the platform then move my legs under the platform to get to the first rung of the ladder. Luckily, my arms weren't tired anymore and the beer had worn off enough for me to focus. Slowly, step by step I made it to solid ground.

Once I let go of the ladder and turned around the woman said, "I didn't think you were Donna."

"No, I'm Carolyn. I just didn't want to get in trouble."

"Well," the woman looked me in the eyes, "if you do it again I will call your father."

"I won't. I promise."

I meant it too. Once was definitely enough.

When we were all about a block away I let my emotions unleash on my friends. I was so pumped up and excited that I wanted to do more crazy things. I wasn't ready to stop now that I had experienced such a rush. My arms and legs felt like electricity was coursing through them and all my worries were far from my mind.

"Let's go see Amy." I said with a renewed energy. "I'm ready for another beer."

Amy was happy to see me again and I happily accepted another beer as I sat on the couch next to Bo. He was in my class but I didn't know too much about him except that he did drugs and was a little edgy which made him a bad boy to hang around. That fit right into my destructive mood and I gave him a smile as I finished off my bottle. It didn't take long for my focus to go from the entire living room to just the little corner that I sat in. The beer was making me tired and the warmth of the house tempted me to close my eyes.

I was trying to talk myself into getting up for some air and to look for Ragan when I felt a hand on my cheek. Bo wasted no time as I turned toward him and quickly kissed me. I knew I should turn away and leave but his lips felt soft and cushy like pillows. The pulse in my neck quickened with every second. I was surprised at his gentleness and how it made me feel like I was in control. I figured I must be drunk because I didn't try to stop as he led me into one of the dark bedrooms. We continued to kiss passionately as his hands surveyed my body. My breathing hastened as he reached the back of my bra and quickly undid the clasp. His hands were warm on my breasts and I started wondering why I wasn't stopping him. It felt like heaven but I knew it was wrong. His lips found my neck, his kisses moved under my ear. My body responded naturally by moving closer, pressing against him. As he unzipped my jeans I decided that would be far enough but instead of moving away I sighed as he reached down and gently rubbed my pelvis. I had no idea another person's touch could feel so overwhelming. Slowly he laid me down on the floor, pulling my jeans and underwear down to my knees.

My mind seemed separate from my body as I contemplated the consequences of what we were doing. My Dad's face came to mind and I tried quickly to replace it with any other thought. He would be furious if he found out what I was doing. Who knew what he would do to Bo. I was sure no one would tell him. Then I thought about God. Well, God is everywhere so obviously He would know. But why should I stop? God didn't seem too concerned about telling the Rev. what was really going on so maybe God doesn't have a problem with it. Just as I was considering letting Bo slide into home base he whispered in my ear, "I love you".

This jolted me back to reality as I placed my hands on his chest pushing him away.

"What did you say?" I demanded.

"I said I love you."

"That's what I thought you said!" I pushed him away. "You don't love me. How could you love me? You barely even know me."

I quickly connected my bra clasps and pulled up my pants.

"Aw Carolyn, please..." he begged. "Don't do this. Come on. You know what I mean."

"No, I don't."

I combed back my hair with my fingers and put on my shoes.

"You shouldn't have told me that."

All of a sudden Christy ran into the bedroom. "Carolyn! Are you in here?"

"Christy? What are you doing here?"

"Carolyn! Come with me right now. If your Dad knew you were here...."

"I don't care. He doesn't know! What do you care anyway?" I was pissed that she thought she could boss me around and she knew it.

"Did he hurt you or force you to do anything?" she asked seriously.

"What?" I was surprised. "No, of course not."

"Okay. That's good. He is the kind of guy that gets what he wants."

"Well, he didn't get it tonight." I was actually relieved.

As we walked out of the house into the cool night air I saw a group of students leaving a school dance. Greg walked up, "So, you did it with Bo huh? Why would you want to lose your virginity to him?"

"I didn't..." I began but he cut me off.

"Yeah, right."

He was mad and walked away before I could respond.

I didn't know if I was more stunned that the word had already spread that Bo and I were doing something or that Greg was mad that it might be true. Either way my virginity was still intact as Christy walked with me back to Ragan's house. My night of dares and destruction had been successful and I was tired.

I half expected that Dad would find out about the water tower and about the party but after a month I realized that parents, especially those that are cops, could be left out of the rumor loop, which was kind of ironic since there were plenty of rumors about him. No one said a word to me about the party either. Greg was mad for awhile and told me that if I was trying to change Bo to make him a better person that I should just give up because it wasn't going to happen. Bo seemed too embarrassed to speak to me so I just chalked it up to a stupid mistake. The realization that I could stop being a goodie-two-shoes without going to Hell or having the world collapse was a huge relief to me. I didn't feel guilty about it either. In fact, I found some satisfaction in the response of others to my actions. I had acted completely out of character and it held their attention. My friends and my high school were becoming more important to me every day and I finally felt like a part of the little town and not just the cop's daughter.

* * * * *

Calmness seemed to settle upon our house and I thought that the rumors had been squelched. Rev. Dewey moved out of state with his family and we went to visit him in his new home. He seemed different somehow, more relaxed. Our new pastor and his young family were welcomed by our congregation but it wasn't easy adjusting to God's new vessel. I could see the honest attempts being made by Cindy and the other faithful churchgoers. It didn't seem important to me. They were strangers and I didn't know how he could possibly reach my soul. I knew the stories in the Bible and I knew how to pray, I just didn't know who to trust. Of course, I trusted Donna but I didn't want to worry her about my sadness. I wanted to protect her from the isolation I was feeling. Dad had been my rock, my hero. He helped baptize me and took us to church. He expected us to be polite young women and not question his decisions. My rock crumbled that night in the car and during Rev. Dewey's prayer it washed out to sea.

Late in November I started noticing that we didn't have the usual holiday spirit around the house. Usually Cindy was singing hymns and baking goodies or working on her quilts. The house was subdued and quiet. No exciting chatter about holiday plans or meals. Finally, one night Dad and Cindy told us that we were moving away from Midwest, into Casper and that Donna and I would be going to spend winter break with Mom in Washington while they packed everything up. By the time we returned, our things would be in the new house. They told us it would be better this way because things were heating up around town. The rumors hadn't died down at all. They had festered. I thought the storm had passed but it was only the eye of the storm. The worst of the winds hadn't even begun to howl and no matter how quickly I built a wall around my soul it wouldn't protect me from what was yet to come.

Chapter 9

Too Much Truth

Soaring above the Earth in an airplane always felt miraculous to me. For a person to sit inside a metal container and race across the horizon, above the highest mountains was an amazing event. As Donna and I were carried on the wings of the giant man-made bird, I gazed through the spongy clouds at the checkered planet below and traced the lines of a highway winding its way through a valley and along a river.

We would be landing in a couple of hours. Even though we were really excited about spending Christmas and New Year's Eve in Washington we were still shell-shocked over the news that we were leaving our school. The "we'll see" answer to our questions of whether we would still be spending time with our friends or whether we would be moving back to Midwest later was not reassuring at all. More unsettling than that was the lack of communication between us and Dad and Cindy. What could be so bad that we would move away from the house that Dad constructed from a tiny little shack to a huge, beautiful home? Why did we need to leave our school in the middle of the year? How could we just start completely over, away from our friends, our school and our church? Why couldn't Dad and Cindy just stay and fight?

As Donna and I munched on airline peanuts we watched the beverage cart make its way toward us. We had flown enough to know that the beverage cart meant we would be hitting some turbulence and this flight was no exception. We smiled at each other as we watched the stewardess hang on to the top of the seats while the plane trotted over bumpy airwaves. Turbulence was like a free fair ride and we giggled as our peanuts jumped around on the trays. It was a relief to laugh.

As we began our descent to Sea-Tac Airport we left our worries among the clouds and the turbulence. When the plane landed we didn't think about leaving our school or moving out of town or people being angry at our father. As we walked from the plane toward the gate we only had one thing on our mind and when we stepped through the gate they were standing there waiting for us. Once everyone hugged we headed to baggage claim and watched luggage slide down a long conveyor belt onto a rotating circular platform. Slowly people began to grab their suitcases and duffel bags. It was interesting to see the different types of bags and suitcase colors and try to match the people to their property. The duffel bags almost always matched up with the young men and the most colorful suitcases belonged to women. Business men had the black suitcases that were the most difficult to tell apart so they would run around trying to match up the tags. My suitcase was light blue and easy to spot on the conveyor. Leroy grabbed our luggage then we all headed to the station wagon. There was a sense of security knowing that we would all pile in the old station wagon and I would be heading back to Olympia scrunched up in the back. The familiarity was a real comfort to us.

Mom didn't ask us any questions about what was going on with Dad so I didn't know if she knew everything but I was relieved not to talk about it. We settled in quickly. Donna was happy to have neighbor friends to hang out with and wasted no time getting them to play Truth or Dare. I was able to relax and spend time with my baby sister, Tara. It was nice not to worry about what people were thinking or saying and to have a sense of celebration in the house. Mom created a magical feeling throughout our home as she sang Christmas songs and made sugar cookies with home-made frosting. I had missed being with her during the holidays and I soaked it all in.

For New Year's Eve our entire family went down the hill to our old neighbor's house. Greg and Linda lived next door to us until they bought a home down the hill. We played with their children and the boy across the street whose parents were also good neighbor friends. I had house-sat for Greg and Linda as well as watched their kids during the summer so we were all pretty close. The parents stayed upstairs and drank their favorite holiday cheer while all the kids hung out down in the basement and played pool. We kept running upstairs to listen to the stories and jokes. As the night grew long the jokes would get more interesting and we could get away with hearing the dirty jokes as long as we didn't laugh too loud.

I was getting tired and sat at the top of the stairs where I could listen to the adults but still watch everything that was going on in the basement. The house was hot and Donna's face was red from all the running around. She was happy... just like during the summer. Suddenly, she and the neighbor kids bounded up the stairs, stopped abruptly at the top and faced me.

Donna was excited as she blurted out, "Carolyn, I want to stay. I don't want to go back. I want to stay here with Mom."

I just stared at her for awhile, trying to make the words sink in.

"Carolyn," she continued, "let's stay. Don't go back. Dad can't make us."

"Donna," I began, my voice a little shaky, "you are just excited because you are having such a good time..."

I knew what I said wasn't true and that Donna had wanted to stay during the summer but I wasn't willing to just accept that she was staying.

"I'm not too excited," Donna stressed, "I do want to stay and you should stay too."

"I can't."

"Come on," Donna pleaded.

"I can't tell Dad that I'm staying. I'm going back. I have to." As I said these words I knew that Donna and I would be separated for the first time in our lives. I couldn't explain to her that I still suffered the guilt of telling Mom that we were going to live with Dad. How could I say that I'm not going to live with him anymore? How could I do to Dad what I had done to Mom? How could I explain to Dad that when things got tough that I baled on him? I wouldn't leave him, especially now that we were getting kicked out of town but it pained me to think of going back alone.

"I'm going to go tell Mom right now." Donna announced. "She will be so happy and she would be even happier if we were both staying."

"I know," I swallowed hard at the thought of going back without Donna, "but I can't."

I held back my tears as Donna made her way into the dining room and told Mom she was staying. My stomach began to hurt and I could feel my face grow pale as I listened to Mom's voice grow excited and everyone cheer. I desperately wanted to stay with Donna but that wasn't going to be enough to make me change my mind. I had no idea how I would handle being without her in Wyoming but I knew she would be happiest in Washington. I didn't try to talk her out of her decision, it was hers to make, and I had a strong sense that things were not going to be better in Casper. The only anchor we had left there was Dad and Cindy but it was clear that the anchor wasn't going to hold in the tidal wave of consequence.

Once again we all stood at the gate in the airport. Only this time I would be the only one getting on the flight. I hugged everyone goodbye and when it was Donna's turn she asked me one more time not to go. I hugged her tight, "I love you."

"I love you too", she cried.

I headed down the ramp toward the plane knowing that I had made a big mistake but had no idea how to fix it.

Soaring above the Earth once again, I closed the window shade and silently allowed tears to cascade down my cheeks. Isolation and loneliness took no time finding me as I wondered what would be waiting for me in Casper. I would ask Dad if I could still go to Midwest for school since some of the teachers made the daily commute. If he said yes to that then everything would probably be okay. I just had no idea how I could live without my sister.

* * * * *

Dad was waiting for me at the airport. "Hey kiddo", he wrapped his arm around my shoulders for a sideways hug; "ready to go check out your new digs?"

"Ya", I answered, "where is it?"

"Not too far from the school."

"Which school?" I asked knowing it could be one of two high schools.

"Natrona. We'll drive by it."

It didn't really matter which school. They were both huge. As we drove by Natrona County High School, the brick tower entrance rose to the clouds. The school was enormous, at least 3 stories high and appeared to take up a full city block.

"Dad, do you think I might be able to still go to Midwest if someone drove me?"

He was silent for a moment then asked, "Who would drive you an hour there and back every day?"

Encouraged by the question I quickly answered, "Mrs. Neal could. She lives here in Casper and I would just ride with her."

I waited as Dad chewed on the inside of his cheek. Finally, he sighed, "It isn't a good idea. Christy's parents are starting a lot of problems for us. They found out she has been talking to us about her home life and now they are making a bunch of stuff up saying that I am trying to tear their family apart. I guess it's easier for them to do that than to pay attention to the problems in their own home."

I didn't say anything in response. The answer to my question was no and that's all I had to hear.

Within a few minutes of the school we were in a residential neighborhood and Dad parked by a white house. It was a nice older house but there was nothing special about it. Once we were inside I noticed how much smaller it was than our house in Midwest but since there were only three of us we didn't need much space. Dad and Cindy's bedroom was on the main floor. To get to my room there was a door in the kitchen that led down a steep wooden staircase into the basement. Dad led me down the stairs and immediately I could feel the temperature cool. It looked like a typical basement with a gray cement floor. To the left there was a bathroom and directly in front of us were two rooms.

"We were going to let you and Donna decide which rooms you want", Dad explained, "but since Donna didn't come back you can pick. We put your stuff in the biggest one thinking that would be the one you would choose."

I looked at both rooms, "The big one will be fine. I like the little window."

Once Dad left me alone to unpack I sat on the edge of the bed and wondered where all my things were. There wasn't much in the room. Cindy had left clean sheets folded up on the bed so I decided that was a good place to start. Then I placed my clothes in the dresser. Still wondering where the rest of my stuff was, I walked over to Donna's room and started to ask her if all her things were in her room before I remembered she wasn't there. I stopped at the doorway, unable to go all the way into her room. Every part of my body knew that she was far away. I leaned against the door jam and wondered what she was doing. I wanted her to be there sitting on her bed complaining about the basement but happy that our rooms were side-by-side. Suddenly a phone rang and I jumped, letting out a little scream. Between the two bedrooms there was a little stand with a beige phone on it. I could hear Cindy answer the phone upstairs and then her footsteps on the kitchen floor moving toward the basement door.

"Carolyn, honey", she called down, "your sister is on the phone. Go ahead and pick it up down there."

I grabbed the receiver and quickly said, "Hello?"

The deep voice on the other end thundered through the phone, "Hellooooo! It's me. Are you okay?"

I smiled at the phone, "I am now."

* * * * *

The first week in the new house brought sleepless nights as I prepared myself to be the new kid in class once again. It became obvious how much I relied on Donna as my sounding board and the smaller room that was to be hers grew more ominous and empty every time I walked past it. Dad and Cindy spent a lot of time in their bedroom talking and Dad wasn't getting up as early as he used to. He was on some kind of leave from work so I had no idea where he went during the day.

I had snuck a carton of cigarettes into my suitcase that I bought in Washington and found that I could smoke a couple at night without Dad and Cindy finding out. They couldn't smell it since they were smokers and I was careful to hide them. They never came down into the basement so the chances of getting caught were slim. During the day I would go for walks and smoke freely as I checked out the route I would take to school. There was no one to talk to as the weight of depression drug me down as I made my way through the neighborhood.

Cindy drove me to school the first day and filled out the paperwork. I met with the counselor to sign up for classes and was immediately disappointed the classes I took in Midwest were not available. Then there was a problem with determining what level of Math to put me in. I signed up for Advanced Biology and ended up with basic P.E. I hoped to make friends at the new school since there were so many students. Cindy knew a few girls that went there and asked them to show me around on my first day. One of the girls, Bethany, was Cindy's cousin's daughter or some distant relative I didn't know. They promised to be in the cafeteria at lunch to meet up with me. Until then I had to navigate my way around 4 different floors that were shaped in a square with a courtyard in the middle. I was late to every class.

In Biology I sat with a couple of smart boys that were a little on the nerdy side. They were sweet and more than helpful getting me up to speed on the current project. Geometry was way over my head since I was joining the class in the middle and hadn't had the opportunity to learn the lessons from the beginning. When lunch time finally arrived it took me ten minutes to get to the cafeteria but Bethany was waiting for me as promised. She had two friends with her and they invited me to sit at their table. I set my tray down across from them and immediately noticed that they didn't have a tray. Bethany informed me that they didn't eat the gross cafeteria food and besides that they were watching their weight and cafeteria food makes you fat. I thanked her for the heads-up and picked at my tray. I wouldn't be eating lunch and wondered where I had seen the vending machines. Then Bethany and her friends started gossiping about some other girl while they each pulled out their make-up bags. I watched in awe as they applied mascara, eyeliner and lipstick while talking the entire time. My head began to throb as their voices grated on my nerves. I had to be polite and act interested but my instinct to flee made it difficult. I wouldn't be going to the cafeteria for lunch again unless I changed my schedule so it could be at a different time.

Finally it was time for P.E. and I was ready to let out some aggression. I rushed to the locker, changed into my P.E. clothes and ran to the gym. I was the last one there. How did these students get to class on time? The teacher began reminding everyone of the rules. As I listened it became apparent that I had signed up for the wrong class. We would not be playing team handball or dodge ball. Nothing like that at all. Instead we would be doing calisthenics and badminton. I glanced around me and took in my peers. They were generally small and thin with little to no muscle mass. I was the biggest in the class. However, instead of being negative about it I thought that it was my chance to be the best in the class. Maybe I could even be an assistant of sorts.

After the first week I started walking to and from school. I decided to change P.E. classes after all and met with my counselor. I was able to get into an advanced P.E. class and take a 6th period study hall which changed my lunch time. I went back to eating cafeteria food instead of vending machine snacks but I sat alone. I received a "C" on my first Biology assignment which was shocking since I had been receiving an "A" at Midwest. I completely flunked the weekly Geometry test because I blanked out and couldn't even think of my name. I walked up to the teacher and handed him the blank test and walked out the door. I had never failed a test. The P.E. class was super hard. There were seven Amazon girls in the class and myself running around an indoor rubber track. We just ran in circles and lifted weights. I was the slowest of the group but I ran until I was exhausted and on the verge of hyperventilation every time.

After the third visit with my counselor to change classes he suggested I stick with the classes and give them a chance but by then I had given up. I would never fit in to the school and I couldn't keep up with my classes. I had no one to talk to and I didn't want to go home. By the third week I started skipping school all together. I would get ready in the morning and start walking to school just as Dad and Cindy left the house. I walked four or five blocks and then backtracked. I knew I was in trouble as I walked down to my bedroom and smoked cigarette after cigarette. I could feel the dark chill in the basement start to close in on my spirit. I didn't want to flunk my classes. I had been an "A" student in Midwest. I didn't want to lie around and smoke tobacco all day. I had played sports and hung out with friends. Yet here I was. Was anyone wondering about me? Did they all think I knew what was happening with my Dad? Did they think I thought it was okay? What about the church? Where were they now? And what about God? Why was He letting this happen?

* * * * *

It was a Saturday morning when we received a knock at the door. Dad was in his room but said he would get it so I sat down on the living room sofa. Dad talked to Cindy for a minute as the knock came again. I was anxious to answer it but something told me Dad knew who it was. When Dad came into the living room he looked at me briefly and said he would be back in a few hours. Dad turned the knob and opened the door. It was two police officers I didn't know. They had arrived to arrest my father and take him downtown for questioning. Dad quickly stepped out of the house and shut the door. Cindy stayed in her room and the house was silent. I sat on the sofa for a little while longer, staring at the door, before slowly making my way back down to the basement.

As I lay on the bed I wondered what Dad was doing exactly. They were probably taking his finger prints and mug shot but how were they treating him? I imagined they were treating him pretty good. He was a master at manipulation and could make a person believe the world was flat. I knew how he did it because I took after him. All he had to do was make himself believe that his lies were true. It was like acting, only stronger and with more conviction. Once you believed your own lie it had to stay that way. You could never change your mind again. That way the lie stayed the truth and any sense of doubt you might have had would disappear.

I was in bed when Dad came home. I could hear him walk into the kitchen and open the fridge. He was probably pouring a glass of milk. I felt guilty for thinking that his day was easy. He must have been questioned about his entire life and accused of things in front of his own peers. That would be hard and he was probably exhausted. I wished that he would just come talk to me about it and tell me the truth. I hated knowing about the car ride and it made me mad that I had to deal with it. I could still see his hand on Christy's inner thigh moving its way up. How was I ever going to get that out of my head? I said a little prayer, "God, please get that out of my head! I can't stand it. Please make Dad tell Cindy the truth. Please God. Let the truth out. In Jesus' name, Amen."

The house was starting to feel like a prison or a mortuary. No one was talking and the silence was suffocating. Dad walked back across the kitchen floor. I could hear his footsteps going into the living room. He was going to watch television. I pictured his socked feet crossed at the ankles on the coffee table and his left elbow on the arm of the sofa, gnawing on the inside of his cheek as he considered the events of his day. How could I ever tell Donna any of this? I was glad she wasn't here. It would tear her apart and she would probably try to confront Dad about it. She was no match for Dad, I was sure of that. So much for blood being thicker than water.

I slept in on Sunday morning since we weren't going to church. Cindy said we would find a new one but it didn't seem like anyone was looking. As I lay in my bed I could hear Cindy talking to someone. The only visitors we had since moving in to the house were the police officers. The muffled voice sounded like a woman so I crawled up the basement stairs and peeked under the door. All I could see was the bottom of the counter and a piece of lint on the kitchen linoleum. I turned my head sideways so my ear was turned toward the door. When I heard the woman's voice again I recognized it. It was Jenny! Cindy's best-friend had come to see her. I opened the door and walked into the utility room to greet her. Cindy quickly stopped in mid-sentence as I said hi. Jenny smiled but didn't pursue a conversation with me so I turned back to the kitchen.

I walked out to the living room to make it seem like I had something to do and then back to the kitchen to get a glass of milk. I could hear the tone of their words which were hushed and intense. As I pulled the milk jug from the top shelf of the refrigerator I heard Cindy say that no matter how hard she prayed that Satan kept bringing doubt into her heart. She questioned whether she was a good Christian and had enough faith. Jenny assured her that she was a good Christian woman and asked her to consider whether it really was Satan making her doubt her husband or whether it was God trying to speak to her. I poured my milk and quickly put the jug back as Cindy became upset and told Jenny to leave. Jenny started to plead with her as I gulped down half my milk.

Cindy set down her tea cup and quietly yet directly, told her best friend that she believed in her husband and that if Jenny didn't believe in him then they didn't have anything else to talk about. As Jenny got up to leave she glanced my way with a look of sadness and pity on her face. I wanted to run after her and tell her that I knew it was God and not Satan. I wanted to tell her that I had proof and had seen with my own eyes that there was reason to doubt. I wanted to ask her to take me with her back to Midwest. Instead, I rinsed out my milk glass and walked back down the stairs into the basement.

In less than a month my grades had dropped from A's to C's or worse. I was surprised that the school hadn't tried to contact anyone about my absences but with over a thousand students to deal with they probably didn't even know I was missing or maybe I was there just enough to keep from being noticed. I decided to go in and talk to my counselor about getting some counseling but when Monday morning came I could barely walk. I had started my period. The pain in my legs and the abdominal cramps were so bad I started to cry. I could feel my face going pale as I hunched over and made my way across the basement floor to the bathroom. I was afraid I would pass out and hit my head on the cement as sweat started pouring from my face. By the time I made it to the toilet my body was shaking uncontrollably from chills. My underwear was blood-soaked and as I started to yell for help everything went dark. When I woke up my head was between the back of the toilet and the wall. I had no idea how long I had been passed out but my whole body was cold and wet from perspiration. I cleaned myself up and slowly made my way back to bed. I missed my Mom.

The week went by slowly. I stayed down on my bed in the basement and wrote letters when I wasn't in school which was most of the time. I wanted to write down how I was feeling but every time I tried it wasn't right. Dad and Cindy didn't check on me in the evening so I smoked in-between attempts at writing. I had about half a carton of cigarettes left which would last me a couple weeks if I rationed them. There was no point in going upstairs since there would be no one to talk to anyway. I thought I might go for a walk in the afternoons to get some fresh air and talk to God outside. When I talked to Him in the basement it felt like my thoughts were bouncing off the ceiling and back at me. Outside it was different. I could feel my thoughts going straight up into space.

I thought about talking to Ragan but didn't want to burden anyone else with what I was going through. I wadded up the notebook paper with my latest attempt at figuring out my feelings and threw it in the corner of my room. Frustrated, I stood up and walked across my room to the closet when the phone rang. It was probably for Cindy. I grabbed my jacket from the hanger and reached for a partial pack of smokes from the dresser. I headed out of my room right as Dad opened the basement door.

"Carolyn", he called down.

"Ya", I answered back trying not to sound annoyed.

Dad's voice was quiet as he replied, "Christy is on the phone and she wants to talk to you."

So many thoughts were going through my mind as I walked toward the stairs. Why did Christy call the house? Did she know that Cindy was home? Did she know Dad had been arrested? What could she possibly want to talk to me about? I doubted she wanted to talk about my new school. As I started to climb the stairs Dad told me I could use the phone in the basement which surprised me even more. I thought for sure that he would want to listen to my conversation with Christy, in case there was something he could use in his defense or to keep her from telling me the truth. He must know exactly what she was about to say, otherwise he wouldn't let me talk with her.

I walked to the phone and picked up the receiver, "Hello?"

"Carolyn?" Christy almost whispered my name.

"Ya?" I couldn't hear very well as the pulse of my heart beat loudly on my ear drums.

"Are you okay?"

"I'm fine." I lied as anger and frustration started to surface. Why did she wait so long to call me?

"Are we still friends?" Christy's voice sounded concerned and sad.

I was silent for a moment. Was she serious? Maybe she was trying to get information out of me for her case. I wondered if Dad was on the phone listening. I didn't think he was but I couldn't be sure. Were they trying to find out what I really knew? I heard Christy's voice again, "Carolyn? Are you still there?"

Quickly I blurted, "Do you really want to be my friend? Were we really ever friends?"

"Yes, I want to be your friend!"

"Then prove it", I answered back, "tell me the truth and we can still be friends."

"You don't want to know everything."

"Yes, I do", I demanded.

"Okay. I'll tell you everything."

"I mean it Christy. Tell me everything or our friendship is over forever." I was surprised at my ultimatum and couldn't decide if I was bluffing.

"I will tell you everything. I've wanted you to know for a long time", Christy said with what almost sounded like relief in her voice.

If Dad had been listening he surely would have made me get off the phone. I listened for his footsteps across the kitchen floor but there was silence. He wasn't rushing to pull the phone cord out of the wall. He wasn't getting on the other line to tell Christy to be quiet. The five seconds it took for Christy to begin her confession seemed like days as I tried to prepare myself for the unknown. The fine hairs on my arm stood up as adrenaline raced through my veins with each thundering boom of my heart. Finally, I would know the truth whether I liked it or not. Finally, I would know if my instincts had been right. Finally, there would be no more secrets.

* * * * *

Slowly, Christy started from the beginning, taking us all the way back to her innocence... she was barely thirteen years old. My father would have been right around 32 or 33 years old and married to Cindy at that time. Dad was Christy's Sunday School teacher then and she would go to the house to talk about the lessons. She was having problems at home with her parents and both Dad and Cindy were easy to talk to about things. She felt comfortable around Dad and thought he was really handsome. I wasn't surprised by any of the story so far. It was a typical crush that I had seen in many young girls' eyes when they would gaze at my father. But then she went on with her story.

Christy started coming by the house when she knew Dad would be home alone. She admittedly would make up stories just so she could see him. She was amazed at how smart he was and would listen to him talk about everything from the planets to microscopic cells. He told her his big dreams and dared her to dream big with him. She wanted to learn everything from him. He was romantic and made her feel special and beautiful at a time when she was invisible to her parents. He was gentle with her and she was in love. Christy felt guilty for loving my father because she liked Cindy a lot but she couldn't stop seeing him, especially once they started having sex. Dad had been her first, she had lost her virginity to him and she wanted to always be with him. She even hoped that some day, when she was old enough, they would get married.

Christy paused for a moment to let this sink in. I couldn't decide how to feel. My emotions were mixed. I knew she had lost her virginity at 13 years old, I had done the math before, but I could never have guessed it was to my father. Christy was only one year older than me. And why did everyone think they were going to marry my Dad? I tried to picture Christy as my new step-mother, there was no way.

In an effort to get a grip on what she was telling me I asked where they had done it. She said there were too many times to count but she could give examples of times I could have caught them.

"Remember when your Dad took me down in the basement to see your Christmas gifts?" Christy paused so I could think back.

I quickly recalled how I was upset that she saw our gifts and how I decided that Donna and I would sneak a peek at them to make up for it.

"Well," she confided, "I had already seen your gifts before. Do you remember seeing the little bench down there?"

I thought back to how the basement had looked with unwrapped gifts strewn about and a small bench placed a little off to the left. I had thought it was to be used as a surface for wrapping presents.

"The bench was so we could stay off the floor."

I grimaced at the vision that was forced into my mind. I knew what she was saying was true but it was still difficult to hear it out loud. Christy gave me a few more examples of times that I would remember so that I would have no more doubts about their relationship. They were together at the hotel when I knocked on the door and they were together the night I saw Dad's hand on her thigh. The time I came home sick with the fever Dad had expected Christy but had to change plans at the last minute when I showed up. She reminded me about Dad's work schedule and how he could be at home anytime he wanted or take a ride out into the county on the many dusty roads that seemed to lead to nowhere.

All of a sudden I started to put it together. There had been many times Christy was at my house when I came home. She would say she was waiting for me or that she needed to talk with Dad about something. I had always thought I was the one that had introduced Christy into our family home when we became friends. Little did I know she had been coming to my home for a couple years before that.

"When you moved in with Ed and Cindy," she began, "he asked me to be your friend. I didn't want to do it because it seemed kinda mean but he kept asking so I said I would. So when you started going to school I made a point of being your friend. Remember when I came up to you in the hall? But Carolyn I really did become your friend. Once I got to know you I really liked you. You are a lot like your Dad. You were easy to talk to and accepted me. That's what made it hard when you saw what was going on in the car that one night. I didn't want to lose you as a friend and I really meant that."

I started to feel uneasy on the phone. It was too much information at one time but now that Christy had opened up to me she let it all out. She went on to talk about her intimacy with my father and how he enjoyed her willingness to try new things. He discussed ideas and desires with her that he wouldn't share with anyone else, not even his own wife.

"He told me one time," she said, "that he wished he could raise a daughter that he could have sex with, without her thinking it was wrong."

"That's gross!" I responded. I decided I wasn't going to believe her and tried to erase the words from my memory. I wanted the sound of that sentence out of my ears and back in her mouth. Why would she even say such a thing to me? Even if it were true why would she tell me of all people? I didn't need to know about their twisted talks and perverted ideas.

"I'm just telling you because I said I would tell you everything."

"Well, I don't need to know everything. You've told me enough."

We had been on the phone for quite awhile so Christy, being convinced that I had enough information about her relationship with my father, changed the subject to Dad's arrest.

"They want to talk to me about Ed," her voice had clearly changed to fear. "My mom is pushing me to tell the truth about everything but I can't. I love him."

"Tell the truth."

I knew the truth would destroy my Dad but the lies were destroying much more. Christy had only been 13 years old. Now she had sex with almost anyone it seemed. She took drugs and drank. She seemed way too old for her age and didn't fit in anywhere. I knew this was all thanks to my Dad.

Christy wouldn't consider it. "I can't. He would go to jail and I wouldn't be able to see him. He is going to meet me this week and help me to pass the lie detector test. He says there's a drug you can take to help you pass and he is going to help me figure out how to answer the questions. Then I won't get so nervous."

"Christy, please just tell the…"

"I have to go now," Christy interrupted, "my Mom just got here."

"Okay."

"Are we still friends?"

"Yes, we are still friends."

"I'm glad I told you everything."

"Me too," I lied. "Bye."

I hung up the receiver and drug my jacket along the floor as I turned back to my bedroom. I didn't want to go upstairs and chance seeing my father now. My eyes were too revealing and he would know that Christy spilled her guts. Maybe he told her to tell me but why would he do that? Who was my father anyway?

* * * * *

Chapter 10

Night's Carnivore

The beach at dark
terrifies me.
The Ocean, monstrously
preys on the sand.
I can hear it grumbling.
Only moments ago the
Sun set on its back
melting over the horizon.
Or did the Ocean
swallow the Sun?
I can't know for sure.
No one promised tomorrow.

~Carolyn A. Ames

I cried into my pillow for an hour before turning onto my back to stare at the ceiling. Everything Christy said was whirling around in my head and I felt nauseated. The basement door opened and I quickly sat up, kicked my cigarette carton under the bed and closed my notebook. Cindy stopped at my bedroom doorway and looked around at my room. Was she going to ask me about the phone call? Did she know who it was? What would I say if she asked? Instead she just smiled bleakly and said dinner was ready. We were having spaghetti. She turned back toward the stairs and I desperately wanted to call her back to me. I wanted to tell her the truth, not just for her sake but for mine. I needed someone to talk to, an adult. But instead, I watched her climb the stairs and go through the door to the kitchen.

As I sat at the table I placed my napkin on my lap. Cindy said our prayer and I began dishing up my spaghetti. I wasn't hungry at all but I didn't want them to think anything different was going on with me. We ate in silence. After dinner Dad went to the living room to watch a TV mini-series called ShoGun and Cindy went into the sewing room. After finishing the dishes I went into the living room and sat by Dad on the couch. It was hard to tell if he was really watching the show or thinking about other things. I wanted everything to rewind back to me not knowing anything, back to us being in Midwest with Donna and back to singing in church. After 20 minutes I went into the sewing room to see Cindy but she had already gone to her room and the door was shut. I could hear her talking on the phone so I quietly walked closer to the door. She was talking about Dad's arrest, saying that he was charged with a couple counts of statutory rape of a minor and several counts of drug charges. I heard her mention Christy's name and that she didn't understand why she would lie when they had helped her so much. My body stiffened as I felt the blood drain from my face. Fearing I would faint I quickly ran down into the basement and to my room.

I wasn't quite sure what statutory rape meant but the word rape was a raw and undeniable word that made me think of a man forcing a woman to have sex by beating her up until her face was bloodied and swollen. Dad wasn't a rapist, he was an adulterer. He didn't beat Christy up; she enjoyed having sex with him. How could that be considered rape? In the old days they would have marked Dad's forehead with a big red letter A and called it good. If he lived in Utah as a Mormon it would have been accepted. But we weren't Mormons and we didn't live in Utah.

I had no idea what the drug charges were about and figured that someone must be trying to set him up for being a cop. Dad had spent time teaching us to stay away from drugs. He even had samples in baggies to show us what the drugs looked like and index cards describing what they would do to us if we took them. Was he turning around and providing them to Christy? She said on the phone that he knew of a drug to help her pass the lie detector test and I did remember a night when he came home with glassy red eyes after being out with some of the cadets. I thought he had been drinking and I decided to continue believing that until someone could prove otherwise.

The more I thought about Cindy being in her room upstairs talking to someone about Dad's innocence, the more I knew I had to tell her the truth. I respected Cindy as a good Christian woman.

She did everything right. She went to church every chance she could, cooked nutritious meals, sewed clothing, went to work 40 or more hours a week and made our house a home. She did everything she thought Dad wanted, including raising his daughters. She didn't deserve to be deceived. She needed to know that God was trying to get through to her.

As if on cue, Cindy came down stairs to put away some clean towels. Quickly, before I lost my nerve, I walked to the entrance of my room.

"Cindy, can I talk to you for a minute?"

"Sure, honey, what is it?"

I walked back to my bed and we both sat on the edge. My heart was racing as I rung my hands together anxiously. I looked down at the floor trying to summon enough courage to tell her the truth. I couldn't tell her everything. It wasn't my place to do that and I couldn't prove what I hadn't seen for myself, even if Christy told me directly. It would just be her word against Dad's word. So all that was left to tell was what I had seen with my own eyes. Hopefully that would be enough.

"I have to tell you something." I took a deep breath and exhaled heavily. "It's about Dad." There was no going back now.

Cindy's face tightened and her jaw set. I had never seen this expression from her but I was convinced that I was doing the right thing and I was determined now to follow through no matter what the consequence.

"Carolyn, what is it that you have to say to me about your Dad?"

Cindy's tone was defensive. I had not considered that she might get mad at me. I had never lied to her or given her a reason not to believe me but I also knew that I was no match for Dad.

"I saw Dad put his hand on Christy's thigh when we were driving back from one of the quiz shows."

I looked Cindy in the eyes.

"They thought I was asleep...and he put his hand on her knee..."

Cindy grabbed my hand and pulled me toward the door.

"Come with me right now...we are going to hear what your Dad has to say about this."

I had a hard time keeping up with her. She had a good grip on my hand as we climbed the stairs. I had no idea what to expect but I knew it wasn't going to be good. I thought Cindy would talk to me about it and maybe reassure me that she already knew about the incident and that everything would be okay. But, instead, we were barreling through the kitchen and into the living room. She stopped abruptly in front of the couch where Dad was sitting, still watching ShoGun with his feet crossed on the coffee table.

"Your daughter has something to tell you!"

Cindy was screeching now and fear climbed into my throat, threatening to choke me to death.

Dad was alarmed at Cindy's odd behavior and in an effort to calm her down he kept his voice quiet.

"Carolyn," he said, "what do you want to tell me that has Cindy so upset?"

Shocked that Cindy had forced me into the position of confronting my father I stood frozen in place.

Cindy was in hysterics as she demanded I tell my father what I had told her. I tried to swallow but my mouth and throat were dry. I shifted from one foot to the other. I couldn't look at him as I repeated what I had told Cindy.

"I saw you and Christy in the car that night we were coming back from the quiz show. You put your hand on her thigh..." I could barely get the words out as my stomach tightened.

"I don't know what you think you saw..." Dad's voice was slow, pronouncing each word as if I were deaf.

"I know what I saw. It's true and you know it." Did I just say that? I couldn't believe what I was hearing myself say. I was swaying slightly and could feel my legs shaking. Darkness was forming around my vision like I was in a tunnel and I thought I might pass out. Dad didn't move from the couch. Instead he made me move forward a little so he could see me clearly. I took two steps toward the coffee table so I was in his direct line of vision, parallel to the television. As I looked at him my vision was out of focus so I didn't have to look into his eyes. I wouldn't need to. His facial expression was one of pure disgust.

"I expected more from you Carolyn. Your disloyalty makes me sick."

I didn't say another word and, after what seemed like a lifetime, I was dismissed to my room to think about how I had dishonored my father and my family. I didn't know how my legs actually carried me down the stairs but once I got to my room I collapsed on my bed and cried until there were no tears left.

I slid off my bed and onto my knees to pray like a child. Putting my hands together and closing my eyes I prayed hard for God to tell me what I had done wrong. Cindy's actions and Dad's words kept swirling around in my head and interrupting my prayer so I prayed out loud. I needed God to hear me.

"Dear God, what did I do wrong? I'm so sorry for not doing it right. Why did Cindy do that to me? Why doesn't she believe me? Please tell her it's all true. Please! I don't know why she would think I made it up. Dear Lord please help Dad. Please make him like he used to be. Please forgive him for his sins."

I opened my eyes and peered up at my ceiling. Nothing. I could feel resentment building up inside me as I spoke. "God, why don't you hear me? You are supposed to be everywhere all the time so why aren't You here now?" Frustrated, I punched my mattress and lay on the cement floor. I could see my cigarette carton under the bed, my notebook and a bookmark. Reaching under the bed I grabbed the bookmark and blew off the dust. It was a picture of Jesus. I turned it over and read the back. It was titled The Beatitudes, Matthew 5:3-12.

3 "Blessed *are* the poor in spirit,
   For theirs is the kingdom of heaven.
4 Blessed *are* those who mourn,
   For they shall be comforted.
5 Blessed *are* the meek,
   For they shall inherit the earth.
6 Blessed *are* those who hunger and thirst for righteousness,
   For they shall be filled.
7 Blessed *are* the merciful,
   For they shall obtain mercy.
8 Blessed *are* the pure in heart,
   For they shall see God.
9 Blessed *are* the peacemakers,
   For they shall be called sons of God.
10 Blessed *are* those who are persecuted for righteousness' sake,
   For theirs is the kingdom of heaven.

11 "Blessed are you when they revile and persecute you, and say all kinds of evil against you falsely for My sake. 12 Rejoice and be exceedingly glad, for great *is* your reward in heaven, for so they persecuted the prophets who were before you.

I read the 9 blessings that were listed and got up off the floor. The bookmark must have fallen out of my Bible. I took my Bible from the dresser and sat back on my bed. Once I found the book of Matthew I placed the bookmark amongst all the red type which indicated Jesus' words. The New Testament was my favorite and there were many verses underlined in pen. Turning to the front of my Bible I read what Cindy had written on the inside flap.

> *Dearest Carolyn,*
> *I hope you always*
> *treasure this book, not just*
> *because it is a pretty Bible but*
> *because it is God's word.*
> *Dad and I are proud to*
> *have a Christian daughter like*
> *you and no matter what happens*
> *we will always love you and*
> *pray for you.*
> *Truly may the Lord*
> *richly bless you and may your*
> *life always be a testimony to others!*
> *Love –*
> *Mom & Dad*

The date on the second page was May 14, 1981, my 14th birthday. Things had changed so much since then. I doubted that they were praying for me now. I thought back to the four of us sitting in the second row at church. I had thought we were so upstanding back then, the perfect Christian family, but we were just as hypocritical as the others. Placing my Bible back on the dresser I crawled between the sheets, turned off my lamp and tried to sleep. I tossed and turned all night, worrying about what the morning would bring but also fearing the desperate thoughts that are made real in the night.

The next morning no one called down from the basement door to wake me up or talk to me. The house was silent. I quietly tiptoed up the stairs in my bare feet and peeked under the door. They were either still asleep or gone and since they were early risers I guessed that they were gone. Not wanting to come face to face with either Dad or Cindy I waited a little longer, until my feet were freezing, and then slowly opened the door. Sticking my head out first, I listened for any sound of life in the house. There was nothing. I gingerly walked around the house to be sure they were gone then poured a cup of coffee. It was still warm so they hadn't been gone long.

I loathed the house I was in. It wasn't' a home at all. There was nothing in the house that was comforting or familiar. What had happened to all our stuff? Dad must have sold it when they moved us out of our home in Midwest. Without warning I started crying again. My face distorted as I let out a wail. It wasn't fair that this was happening! I didn't ask for any of this! I even left Donna in Washington to come back here! I dumped out my coffee and put the mug in the dishwasher. My stomach was too upset for coffee. Deciding that a shower might make me feel better I went down to my room to grab clothes out of my dresser but the feeling of despair was so great that I just lay on my bed. My eyes were puffy and my sinuses were clogged from all the crying. There were no more tears so I just laid there staring at the cement wall in a daze.

I had fallen asleep and didn't awake until the evening. I could hear Cindy running water and getting dinner ready. The television was on so Dad was home. His mini-series wouldn't start until a little later. I got up and went to the bathroom to pee then looked at myself in the mirror. I looked horrible. My eyes were red around the rims with dark circles underneath. My skin seemed pale which made the contrast in color even more noticeable. I splashed my face with cold water and quickly drew in a breath. While dabbing the water off with a towel I heard the basement door open. I froze instantly. Whose footsteps would they be? What would they say? Instead of footsteps I heard Cindy's voice.

"Carolyn. Dinner." There was no emotion just a flat tone.

I was starving but couldn't bear to face my father; or Cindy for that matter. They considered me a traitor and I was getting what amounted to the parent version of the silent treatment.

I went back to my room and brushed my hair. Maybe Cindy would come down and coax me up to dinner then I could talk to her and try to make her understand that I wasn't trying to ruin her life. Maybe I could apologize and she could talk to Dad. After 20 minutes of waiting I heard the door open again. This time there was no voice or footsteps, just the door opening and then closing. As I walked toward the stairway I could see something at the top. It was my dinner.

Chapter 11
Against God's Will

I carried my plate to my bed and started nibbling on the chicken. Cindy had warmed it up in the microwave and it was good. She must not hate me if she warmed up my food. Then again, she wasn't really allowed to hate, she was supposed to forgive. I was surprised that I could be hungry when my life was falling apart. I couldn't remember a time that I couldn't eat a meal unless I was deathly sick. I watched my peas roll around the plate and stop at the side of my mashed potato mountain. I ate my peas one at a time. My arms felt so weak, it was an effort just to lift the fork to my mouth. When I finally finished dinner I carried the plate back to the top of the stairs and listened under the door. No one was in the kitchen. Slowly, I opened the door and set my plate and fork on the kitchen floor. Closing the door back up I turned and went back down the stairs. If Cindy wanted me to wash my plate she could come and tell me to do it.

I wondered what Donna was doing. It was Saturday night so she was probably running around outside with the neighbor kids. It would be cold and dark in Washington and chances were pretty good that it was raining but that never stopped us from going outside. Maybe she had a friend over and they were watching movies or playing a game. She would cry if she saw me in the basement and tell me to leave. I wanted to leave but had no idea how I could.

I was so stupid for coming back. I should have known better and now I was getting what I deserved. I thought back to the day I told Mom that Donna and I wanted to go live with Dad because she and Leroy drank too much. Mom and Leroy fought all the time and we knew it was because of the beer. They would party and have fun until they drank too much. Then they would fight about everything. I hated listening to them yell at each other and fight about us. Sometimes they would break dishes or we would have to get dressed and leave. So, there we were, standing by Mom as she lay in her bed reading. Donna just stood and cried while I told Mom we wanted to leave. Mom cried and asked us if we would stay if they quit drinking and we said yes, but when she talked to Leroy about it he had said no. No one was going to tell him what he could and couldn't do and after a long day of work he was going to drink his beer.

Living with Dad was exactly how I had pictured it at first. He was my hero. He saved lives and caught criminals, he prayed and he sang. Cindy made us clothes and taught us all the things she thought we needed to know as young women. We loved our school and had fun but always, in the back of my mind, I carried the guilt of leaving Mom. It was easy to rationalize it when everything was going great but it surfaced every time we went to Mom's house for the summer. She is the one I betrayed. She loved us unconditionally and I didn't think that was enough. I didn't love her unconditionally back. What an idiot I was!

I didn't deserve to go back to Washington. Donna followed my lead and I led her down the wrong path. What kind of sister does that? I left my baby sister, Tara, to grow up without me, her Sissy. The tears were flowing as I realized how horrible I had been to leave them. I was a selfish, inconsiderate person. No wonder God wasn't listening to my prayers, I didn't deserve God. And then, when I had the chance to stay, I denied Mom again. I felt like throwing up as the hatred for myself grew with each passing second. Looking around the cold concrete basement it became clear to me that I deserved to be there, alone. I wanted to die.

I looked at my notebook. All my failed attempts at writing were either wadded up in a ball in the corner of my room or in the notebook with lines crossing out the phrases that didn't quite make sense. I would try one more time. I placed my pencil on the first line of a new sheet of paper. Not a single word came to my mind. Nothing could describe the despair I felt. Nothing could describe the loneliness that cloaked me. Slowly, I started to consider an option to escape my misery. I could kill myself. I had never considered suicide and was mildly curious at my lack of concern. Why didn't I care that I was thinking about suicide? It didn't really matter.

Contemplating my options, I thought about how I could do it. Looking at my pencil, I wondered if it would work as a weapon. The lead point was sharp but was it sharp enough to go through my skin? The yellow wooden pencil was long enough but was it strong enough not to break? I pictured myself stabbing the pencil through my juggler vein. The juggler wasn't very far into my body. It probably wouldn't hurt that much and I would bleed to death pretty quickly if the pencil didn't break off and I didn't miss. I would have to pull the pencil back out before it would work though and my tendency to faint might make that impossible. What if I hit my windpipe? Then I might drown in my own blood, gagging and sputtering. It would be slow and really messy. If I lived I would probably get lead poisoning and have to go through a lot of medical care. I didn't want to be even more of a burden than I was already proving to be. I set the pencil and notebook down on my bed. No, the suicide-by-pencil idea wasn't a good one.

I started pacing the basement floor from my room to the steps and back. I was tired and wanted it to all be over. I didn't care what my Dad did or didn't do. I didn't care that Cindy was going to believe anything he said no matter what. I was done. I was sure that suicide was the answer if I could just figure out the right way to do it. I didn't want anyone to have to clean up a mess and I wanted it to work. As I glanced around the basement I considered running really fast and slamming my head into the concrete wall. I could do it right now, without even thinking. As if in response, I could feel my calf muscles tighten. My breathing increased as my body prepared to run hard and fast. I closed my eyes and swallowed. This was it, time to die. Just as I started to lift my leg for the run I hesitated. There was no guarantee I could hit it hard enough to kill me, it would probably just knock me out. I pictured myself lying on the cold cement floor against the wall, unconscious with a trickle of blood coming from my head. I'd be alive and in pain, maybe I would even have brain damage and have to be taken care of by Cindy. I could be paralyzed and have to listen to everyone talk about me while I sat in a chair unable to leave. I walked over to the wall and ran my hand along the cold bumpy cement and then turned, leaning my back against it. I would have to think of something else.

There were always the old stand-by suicides of overdosing on pills, slicing wrists and hangings. Where would I even get pills? I didn't know what kind would work best and our medicine cabinets weren't full of prescriptions. If I overdosed on medication I knew chances were pretty good that I would get my stomach pumped and I had heard that was a bad process to go through. I would be stuck in a hospital bed with IVs and having to explain myself to a psychiatrist, which would be impossible to do. I envisioned myself telling the doctor, "hi, my name is Carolyn and I want to kill myself because I'm an idiot and my dad hates me." I also knew that slicing my wrists would only work if I went up the arm instead of across the wrist. My father taught me that one. Now, that would be ironic. But that just seemed like too much work, getting in a hot bath, finding the right area, getting the knife deep enough...not to mention the fainting problem. I would probably faint and then drown. I had a real fear of drowning so that wouldn't work.

Walking back to my room, I spread out on my bed in a stupor. Something kept nagging at me and after a few minutes I realized what it was. I couldn't kill myself no matter how badly I wanted to or how easily I could justify it. Suicide was an unforgivable sin. I wouldn't be able to ask for forgiveness from God if I was dead. So now the question was whether or not I believed in God anymore. If God was around He sure wasn't making much of an impression on me but who am I to deserve impressing? Just because I didn't feel God's presence it didn't mean He wasn't around. In my heart I knew God existed, I had felt it in church. Even if I didn't believe everything in the Bible or what I had been taught in church I still felt the supernatural presence of someone or something more. I didn't believe in God's wrath. Why would God need wrath? If God was all of the things I was taught, such as love and peace, then He couldn't have wrath. Yes, I still believed in God even if He had given up on me. I wasn't sure if I believed in Hell but, not willing to take any chances, I decided not to commit suicide just in case.

My bedroom felt like it was closing in on me. I had to get out of the house, out of the misery no matter what the cost. I couldn't call anyone to come get me. Christy was the only one I knew that could drive and I didn't want to see her. She would want to talk to me about things I didn't want to hear. Anxiety pounded my heart until I couldn't stand being in the bedroom any longer. Grabbing a bag from my closet I stuffed it with some basic essentials. I would run away. If I left right away I could make some distance. A trucker or someone would pick me up and I could lie about who I was and where I was going. Cramming my cigarettes and lighter in the sports bag I set my Bible on top and zipped the bag. It was cold outside so I grabbed a sweater and gloves. They would probably think I headed to Washington so I would head south instead. It would be warmer once I got passed Colorado. If I got hurt along the way then that would be up to God.

I decided to write a note before I left. Sitting back down on the edge of my bed I, once again, had my pencil and notebook. Contemplating what I should write I thought of the events of the last week and began to cry. It all seemed like a dream, a nightmare that I should be waking up from but, instead, it just goes on and on. I wondered how Dad and Cindy would react to my running away. Would they take it seriously or wait another day to see if I came back? I really didn't know how they would act. After the way things had gone during the last month the only thing that became clear to me was that I didn't really know them at all. I did know my Mom though, and I knew my sisters. I pictured Dad calling my Mom in Washington to tell her I had run away. What would he say to her? He wouldn't tell the truth so he would have to make up some story about me. I thought about Mom. She would cry but even worse, she would worry and be afraid for me. My sisters would wonder why I didn't come home to them instead of running off into the night where the wolves and truckers roamed. If I ran away I would hurt my mother again and if something bad happened to me, my sisters' hearts would be broken. I couldn't run away.

As I started unpacking my bag the realization of what I had been thinking in the last few hours washed over me. I had actually wanted to kill myself! My body began to shake as I realized how close I had come to death. My senses were suddenly more acute than they had been in days. I shook off the feeling of despair and walked out of my room. I wasn't going to run away but I was going to leave. Picking up the phone's receiver I dialed my mother's number. As I wiped the tears from my cheeks and chin a sense of urgency came over me as I heard her voice answer hello.

"Mom?" my voice was small and quivering.

"Carolyn?" she asked, "Honey, it's really late. Are you okay?"

"Mom, bring me home."

I barely managed to squeak out the words. I could hear voices in the background. The neighbors were over playing cards.

"Are you okay?" she asked again.

"No, mom." I cried. "I need to get out of here."

Mom didn't question me about what had happened. She didn't need any details. She could hear the tone of desperation in my voice, the details could come later. She quickly told Leroy and their friends that I wanted to come home. Her voice was a strange mixture of fear and happiness. She was afraid of what may have happened to cause my voice to be so desperate but happy that I would be coming home to her. The problem would be one of money. Mom and Leroy couldn't just come up with the cash to buy a plane ticket.

"Honey, we have to figure out how to buy your plane ticket...hang on."

I could hear Greg and Linda's voices but couldn't make out what they were saying to Mom. When Mom came back on the line she told me that Greg and Linda were going to loan them the money for my ticket. Not only that but they had the cash at their house and wouldn't need to wait for a bank to open on Monday.

"I'll call you as soon as we know when your flight will be. Hang in there sweetie."

"Okay." I croaked.

My voice was hoarse and my throat was tight as I tried to hold back a wave of emotions. I had done the right thing. I should never have waited to call my family. They loved me and wanted me home. After saying good-bye I went back to my bed and fell asleep within seconds. I hadn't even pulled back the bedspread or removed my shoes.

* * * * *

The phone rang early on Sunday. Bolting out of bed I raced for the phone but Dad had already answered it.

"Carolyn," he called down, "it's your mother."

"Okay." I hoped Dad didn't hear the shakiness of my voice.

"Hello? Mom?"

As I spoke I also listened for the click telling me that Dad had hung up the receiver.

"Hi Honey."

Mom's voice sounded normal and I heard the click. Dad probably figured she didn't know anything if her voice sounded normal.

"Hi." I answered back.

"Are you okay?"

"Yes. I'm much better today. I got some sleep."

"Oh, good I'm glad you are feeling better. I was up all night, I was so worried. Linda and Greg loaned us the money and we got your ticket. Your flight leaves tomorrow at 8:00 in the morning. It's the first flight out. The ticket will be at the airport. Are you going to be okay until then?"

"I'll be okay. I'll see you tomorrow. I love you Mom."

I could feel relief seeping into my body as I realized I would be on my way to Washington within 24 hours, on a plane and away from the storm.

The next step would be hard. I had to tell Dad and Cindy that I was leaving. I figured I would go straight to Dad since telling Cindy would just put me back in front of him anyway. This time I wasn't going to stand in the living room though. I would tell him on my own turf, in the basement.

My stomach was in a knot as I tried to think of what to say then quickly decided to just wing it. The anxiety of waiting was the worst part. Once I got it over with I could deal with the aftermath. It was reassuring to know that Mom was there for me. Even though she didn't know what was going on she was like a Mamma Bear when it came to her children. She may have been a couple of states away but I could feel her support as I walked up the stairs and breathed deeply. I opened the door and called for Dad to come down, that I had something to talk about. He probably thought I was going to apologize for my behavior. Quickly, I descended the stairs and sat in a chair by the phone stand. Wringing my hands, I could feel my pulse race as Dad came down the stairs. He walked slowly, deliberately. His broad shoulders made him look taller than he actually was and his set jaw showed that he was serious.

He stood in front of me for a moment as my eyes diverted to the floor. The feelings from the day before came rushing back. He spoke first.

"You asked me down here. What do you have to say?"

I didn't hesitate, "I'm going back to Washington."

"If you leave, don't expect to ever come back."

"I am leaving. I'm leaving tomorrow morning."

"Then I have nothing more to say to you."

Dad turned abruptly and went back up stairs. After a few minutes I heard him leave in the car.

I started gathering all of my things and placed my suitcase on the bed. This time I was packing to leave for good, no more summer break or winter break. I set aside the things I would need for the morning and turned to grab a pair of shoes when I saw Cindy in the doorway. I hadn't heard her coming down the stairs.

"Your Dad said that you have decided to go back to Washington."

"I am. There will be a ticket for me at the airport."

"Tomorrow?"

"Yes, my flight is at 8:00am."

"Carolyn, if you go back to Washington there is no turning back."

I didn't say anything.

"If you go back to Washington it is against God's will."

I looked at Cindy then with a questioning expression. How could she know what is God's will? She was grasping at straws.

"I don't think so." I said.

Not knowing what else to say she turned and left.

A small part of me was worried. What if she was right? Maybe I was blowing everything out of proportion and leaving now would be going against God. I would have to take my chances. If God was love and truth then I couldn't be doing the wrong thing. Still, it worried me a little.

Less than an hour went by when Cindy came back down to my room.

"Come up stairs with me."

Taking a deep breath I followed Cindy into the living room.

"Sit on the couch", she instructed.

I looked into her face for some sort of hint at what was to come but her face was unremarkable, blank. I couldn't tell what emotion she was hiding. I sat to one side of the couch and she sat next to me. Hopeful that we were going to have a talk and I could explain how I felt I turned in toward her. She reached forward and took her Bible from the coffee table.

"Carolyn, I told you that if you go back to Washington you will be going against God's will. Now, I want you to sit on this couch and read God's word. I want you to start with Romans. I have marked the scripture that you need to read. Then I want you to sit here and pray to God about what you are doing."

I stared at Cindy in disbelief. She was trying to punish me with God's word? I could read the Bible all day and still know that I was going to leave no matter what. I had lost faith in Cindy's ability to hear God.

"Okay." I said.

With that, Cindy left me on the couch for an hour as I read scripture that spoke of the sin of drinking, that children were to obey their parents, and to trust in the Lord. I could feel the darkness coming over me again as I wondered if I had enough faith or if I had given up too soon. What if God was testing me?

When Cindy came back to the living room I was ready to talk about how I felt and about the scriptures I read but instead of trying to sit down and talk with me she accused me again of going against God. My heart hardened a little as I replied.

"If I am going against God then I guess I'll find out. I'm going to Washington. Dad said I could never come back if I leave but I'm going."

"Then we will be taking you to the airport in the morning."

Cindy shut the Bible and placed it back on the table then walked into her room and shut the door.

I spent the rest of the evening packing up my room the best I could. I wouldn't have my own room or bed in Washington but I was happy to trade it for my sisters. Since I never really committed to the room being mine I didn't have to remove anything from the walls. I mostly had clothes, cassette tapes, and a few pieces of jewelry. Once those items were packed I placed my Bible and the last pack of cigarettes under a pair of jeans and zipped up the suitcase. Done. I sat on my bed and looked around the room. It didn't look like it did when I first moved in. It was much uglier now. It wasn't a place that I could hope, or laugh, or pray. Pulling back the comforter and top sheet of my bed one last time I felt a sense of sorrow. I was mourning the loss of what would never be. It was strange to miss something that hadn't even happened. The things that had been said in this house changed everything. I saw my father as a criminal, Cindy as a desperate woman trying to use religion as a weapon, and I saw myself as a foolish 15 year old that still believed in fairy tales. I turned out the light and pulled the covers up to my chest. Closing my eyes I whispered, "God, help me get through tomorrow. I need you now more than ever. Amen."

Turning on my side I wondered what the morning would be like. What would Dad say? Would they try to stop me?

The morning came quickly, as if the night was only a blink. I shut off my alarm and put it in my suitcase. Once I showered and brushed my teeth, I used two bobby pins to hold back each side of my bangs with a part down the middle. It looked childish but I had already packed my curling iron and I didn't really care. Not knowing what to do next I put my suitcase and purse next to the stairs and waited in the basement. Within five minutes the door opened and Cindy said it was time to go. I carried my suitcase up the stairs, through the kitchen and outside to the car. Dad was in the driver's seat with the car running, looking forward. The trunk was open so I put my suitcase in it and closed it down. I was finally heading to the airport.

The ride to the airport was silent. I watched the landscape fly by my window. It wouldn't be long before I was on a plane and away from the suffocating tension that filled the car. As we pulled into the airport parking area Dad broke the silence.

"Are you sure this is what you want to do?"

His voice had no emotion, no promise of a talk or explanation. He was looking at me through the rearview mirror. I glanced down and clasped my hands together.

"Yes, I'm sure."

He pulled the car up to the front of the airport and we all got out. Dad opened the trunk and Cindy grabbed my suitcase. As she handed it to me Dad told her he was going to go park the car and that we should go inside to the gate and get me checked in.

As Cindy and I walked to the gate neither one of us spoke a word. I thought about how she had used the Bible to try and change my mind about leaving. Didn't she realize that I needed her to talk to me instead of quoting scripture? I needed her to tell me that I should stay because they loved me and would miss me. All I wanted was for her to tell me she had doubts or that she was scared. I could even live with the fact my father was a criminal if only they would be honest with me.

We checked my luggage and walked to the gate. My flight was on schedule and they were already boarding. Where was Dad? It was a small airport with plenty of parking. He should have been at the gate. Slowly, it dawned on me. I looked at Cindy.

"He's not coming back is he?"

Cindy's eyes couldn't lie and I knew the truth. He wasn't planning to say good-bye. I swallowed hard to keep down my emotions just as the airline called for my section to board the plane. Turning toward Cindy for a hug I saw her stand erect. I wasn't going to get a hug. My lips began to tremble so I quickly said good-bye and turned away. I didn't look back again as I went through the gate.

Chapter 12
Treading Water

As the half empty plane taxied down the runway I blinked hard to clear my tears so I could look out the small oval window. I didn't have a window seat but no one was seated next to me so I bucked in near the window. I didn't care about having a view during the flight; I only wanted to check the airport windows to see if Dad had come back. No one was at the windows, not even Cindy. As we began to take-off I turned my head so I could see the airport parking lot. Methodically scanning the rows from front to back I searched for Dad's car but couldn't find it. I began to search again but only got to the third row before the plane banked to the right and all I could see was wing. By the time we straightened back out the airport was behind us and out of sight.

My eyes burned and were red from crying so as the stewardess walked down the aisle I closed my eyes to pretend I was asleep. I didn't want her to wonder what was wrong with me. It was strange enough that I was on the flight by myself and I didn't need any questions. I closed the window shade and reclined my seat. What had happened this morning was still playing through my head. Dad deliberately avoided telling me good-bye even though he was the one that caused everything to happen. Was he still playing the part of being innocent while giving me the part of traitor or was he so sad that I was leaving that he couldn't bear to see me go? It was obvious that Cindy viewed me as the traitor since, even with Dad gone, she wouldn't hug me. No, Dad knew what he was doing. He had to play the part that he created now, especially after chastising me in front of Cindy. He was trying to save his marriage at my expense.

As for Cindy, she had to choose sides; either believe me or believe Dad. If she were to believe her husband then she would be standing by her man and they could fight against evil together. If she were to believe me then she would have to confront her husband. He would question her loyalty and her faith in God. After all, Rev. Dewey had spoke of Dad's innocence in front of the church. She would then have to face her friends and family. Most of all, she would have to admit to herself that her husband had been cheating on her. It was much easier to think of me as a traitor. Maybe she thought I wanted more attention or that I was possessed by the devil. It didn't matter, I didn't hate her. I felt sorry for her. She did not deserve any of it. She was the perfect wife, just as Dad required her to be. Still, I wondered if it was hard for her; if she had struggled to not hug me. I decided to believe that she did struggle and I hoped that her doubts about Dad would someday make sense to her.

After about an hour, the plane landed for a stop in Denver. I didn't have to change planes so I rummaged through the magazine pouch in front of me. There was a barf bag, safety instruction card and the airline's magazine that looked like it was several years old. I missed Donna. As I started thinking about her I could feel the emotions of the last couple of days boiling up like magma from a volcano. The guilt and despair threatened to consume me. I could feel my anxiety increasing fast as I started to take deep breaths. People were boarding the plane so I tried to focus on them, to get my mind thinking of something else. There was an old man and an old woman discussing who would get the aisle seat, a woman trying to stow her carry-on in the compartment above her seat and a man trying to patiently wait for the woman to finish so he could get passed her. They were the typical passengers. I lifted the window shade hoping that the outside activity of luggage carts would busy my mind, anything to get my mind off of Wyoming.

"Excuse me, you're in my seat."
The voice was deep but nice. As I turned to see who was speaking I was shocked to see the aisle completely filled up with college men all wearing matching jerseys. They were big with broad shoulders and shoulder length hair. Most had moustaches and beards or long side-burns. They looked Irish to me and they

were talking loudly and were very spirited. Whatever sport they were playing, they must have won. I looked at the man that spoke to me and just stared for a minute. He had shoulder length wavy brown hair, a moustache and whiskers. His eyes were green and sparkling as he smiled at my lack of words. He tried again.

"Uh, you're in my seat. Do you prefer the window?"

"Oh." I finally found my voice. "Sorry, I'll move over."

"No, you can stay. I prefer the aisle anyway. I can chat with my teammates, aye?"

I looked around him as he sat down. There was a teammate across the aisle checking out his magazine pouch and then in all the seats behind us I could see the rest of the team reclining their seats and buckling the seatbelts. Their jerseys were silver with some black and red. I tuned in to the chatter and wondered where they were from. They all had pleasant accents and it soothed my anxiety.

Once we were up in the air the beverage cart started making its way down the aisle. Once again I began to think about Donna. I turned my head toward the window and watched the clouds as the plane weaved in and out of them like an embroidery needle.

"I'll take a Coors."

The man next to me was ordering a beer from the stewardess. He flipped down the tray in front of him and she placed a small napkin down, then the beer and a plastic cup.

"I won't need the cup" he says.

I ordered a 7-up with ice. Once the beverage cart moved down the aisle I could hear beers being ordered by everyone on the team.

"My name is Steve, what's yours?" Steve asks.

"I'm Carolyn."

"How old are you, Carolyn?"

"I'm 15."

"You look older than 15."

"I feel older."

I wasn't kidding about feeling old but I was surprised that he thought I looked older because with my hair done the way it was and no make-up on I thought I looked younger, around 14 years old.

He looked at me for a minute as if in deep thought before continuing.

"Want a drink of my beer?"

"What?" I knew he couldn't be serious.

"Come on, have a drink. You look like you could use it."

"No, thank you."

He looked disappointed so I asked him about the team.

"We are a Curling team from Canada."

That explained the accent. As the beverage cart made its way back up the aisle he stopped the stewardess and ordered two more beers. Once she passed by he put my folding tray down and placed a beer on it.

"This way you can have your own, aye."

I was both afraid and excited to drink the beer. What if the stewardess asked me for my ID? Why was this man buying me beer when he knew I was only 15 years old? Deciding that I had been through a lot in the past couple of days and that a beer was the least of my concerns, I opened the can of beer and took a sip. It was really cold and went down smooth. Steve was happy to toast to me and clanked our cans together. I laughed and gulped down my beer just in time for him to order us a couple more.

Feeling pretty relaxed and comfortable I asked Steve about Curling. He explained to me that he was a Sweeper and used a broom to sweep ice in front of a 40 pound stone to make it change directions. I laughed and told him to tell me the truth. I didn't believe that there was a sport that required big strong men to sweep with a broom. He assured me that it was true and made his teammate from across the aisle confirm what he had just told me.

Steve then went on to talk about how important it was to hold the broom just right and that pressure and speed made the difference between simply cleaning the ice and scrubbing the ice. I tried to picture the game but once he mentioned something called a hog line I couldn't stop giggling. The beer had gone to my head.

As the beverage cart came through again. The stewardess looked exhausted. When Steve ordered two more Coors the stewardess told him there was no more Coors so he told her it didn't matter what kind of beer but then she snapped at him that they were all out of every kind of beer not just Coors. Not to be discouraged, Steve ordered two screwdrivers and told me that I would like them because they have orange juice in them. I smiled. It felt good that he cared what I might like and wanted to talk to me. It had been a long time since I had a talk with anyone about things other than what my Dad had done.

When our screwdrivers arrived Steve told the stewardess to put the second one on my tray. She tightened her lips and set it on his tray before turning away. He just laughed and handed me the drink. I took a small sip to test the flavor and was very pleased. It tasted way better than beer and I could drink it faster.

Steve leaned toward me with a smile and asked for a kiss. I was flattered that a college man would want to kiss me, especially looking the way I did. As if reading my mind he told me that I was beautiful in an innocent way. I didn't want to be innocent; it had gotten me nowhere, so I leaned in and pressed hard against his lips. He pressed back and I could feel his hard whiskers against my chin as his tongue entered my mouth. I could taste the vodka and orange juice as I ran my tongue along the side of his tongue and over the top. The stewardess walked by and gave us a dirty look. I wondered if she knew how old I was and, if so, why she didn't stop us. We continued to make out for another 30 minutes before being told that the plane was getting ready for its descent into SeaTac. When we stopped kissing my skin was red from his whiskers but I didn't mind. Everything around me was fuzzy. I felt warm inside and wanted to lie down and take a nap.

When the plane landed there were two things I learned right away. It's best if you eat something before drinking a bunch of alcohol and the affects of alcohol intensify when you land. Steve asked for my phone number so I gave it to him but I knew that we could never have a relationship in the real world. He was 22 years old and that was way too old for me. My mom would never allow that. Besides, he didn't know anything about me except how I kissed.

I sat for a minute and watched the old couple slowly merge into the aisle to exit the plane. I wondered how long they had been married and if he had ever cheated on her. I hoped not. As I made my way into the aisle I felt the full affects of the alcohol on my body. I was sluggish and every step was difficult. I tried to clear my head as I walked off the plane and toward the gate. I wondered if Mom would notice anything and then decided that I didn't have the energy to worry about another thing. I really had to pee.

As I turned the corner and walked into the airport my family was waiting right up front for me. I hugged each of them heartedly and when it was time to hug Mom I hugged her for a long time. I missed her. I loved her. I needed her to hold me up so I could rest a minute. After I let go, she looked at me and it was obvious she knew that I had been drinking. When she asked me about it I said that I had a beer or two. She gave me a "who are you kidding" look and we headed to the baggage claim. I heard a whistle and then someone yell my name. We all turned around to see Steve standing by the gate waving to me. I smiled and waved back then stumbled a little. I was truly thankful for Steve. He had gotten my mind off of the worst month of my life with a lot of alcohol, kissing and a lesson about sweeping.

As we headed back toward Olympia it began to rain. Mom had to drive the station wagon to the airport since Leroy was at work and she hated to drive on the freeway. As we passed through Tacoma the traffic was heavy. I watched the rain coming down and realized that I really had to pee. There was nowhere to stop and Mom told me I would have to hold it. I was sure I was going to pee my pants. I spent the next 30 minutes reminding Mom how bad I had to go to the bathroom, while she braved the rain and the traffic all the way home. My sisters just stared at me with confused looks on their faces. Surely they didn't expect me to be drunk when I got off that plane.

* * * * *

Once I was home and settled in, I could feel the difference in my spirit. I was in a place that accepted me for the way I was and I knew how they were. There would be no surprises. Leroy would go to work Monday through Friday, we would all go to school and Mom would stay home doing housework and planning dinner. We would all have dinner together and, if we were lucky, we would have some kind of dessert at 8pm while watching a comedy on television. I shared a bedroom with Donna and slept well at night knowing she was there. No one asked me about what had happened and I knew Mom was giving me my space.

I walked outside on the patio and right into a forest of trees. The backyard was my oasis. I could breathe moist air and fir while feeling protected by the trees and salal. I ran my hand along the rough bark and gazed up over a 100 feet at the tree tops. It was still cold in February but winters in Washington were much milder than Wyoming and the wind was tame.

I started school right away and had a much easier time getting started. It was hard at first to decide what group I should hang out with since Tumwater was so defined by clicks such as the jocks, stoners, nerds and nobodies. I considered being a jock since I loved sports but that required too much of the fake personality. I was drawn toward the smoking area, at first because I wanted to smoke, but it didn't take long to discover that the so-called stoners were extremely accepting of all types-especially if you had cigarettes to share. The classes were easy so my grades would correct within a Trimester and some friends I had made before moving to Wyoming were at the school.

I spent the first two weeks in a daze, trying to move beyond Wyoming. My spirit and emotions had been scattered in the storm and it would take time to pick up all the pieces, sort through them and place everything in order. Just as I thought I was making headway something would happen to set me back.

I had P.E. during my last period and it was nice to take my time getting changed after a workout. It was a Friday and I was the last one in the locker room as I changed. Placing my gym clothes in my bag I sat on the bench that ran the length of the lockers and reached down to tie my shoe. Suddenly, without warning, my mind went blank and I didn't know where I was. I literally didn't know what state I was in, let alone what building I was in. I looked around and nothing was familiar. There were lockers so I was in some kind of gym or at a swimming pool. I didn't feel like swimming was involved though so it must be a gym. I could feel myself panicking as I tried to deduce my location. There was no one around to ask or jog my memory so I started at the top. What state was I in? Wyoming? I didn't think so. It didn't look like Midwest High School and I thought that I had left that school. If I wasn't in Wyoming then where was I? I thought about it for awhile and then it came to me that I was in Washington. Yes, I was in Washington State. I pictured a map of Washington in my head. Okay, so where in Washington was I? Piece by piece I put the puzzle together. I was in Tumwater. I was living with my Mom. I was going to Tumwater High School and I was in the school's gym. I finished tying my shoe and stood up. I would be okay.

When I got home I told Mom about what had happened. It was too scary to keep to myself and she needed to know if her eldest daughter was going crazy. After listening to my story she was concerned and asked me if I thought I needed to see a psychiatrist. I thought about it seriously and then told her that I didn't' need one yet. I would try to work it out with the support of my family and my daily routine. My daily routine appeared boring on the surface but it worked as a baseline to stabilize my unsteady spirit. My internal compass had been tossed about and it would take a little time to find True North again.

It had been barely two weeks since I moved back to Washington when a letter came for me. It was from Dad. My heart beat hard as Mom handed it to me and asked me if I wanted to read it or if I wanted her to put it away for later. I decided to read it outside where I could be alone and concentrate. My head was already feeling blurry and confused and I hadn't even opened it yet. Maybe he was writing to say he was sorry for everything. Why else would he write? I opened the envelope and pulled out a 2-page letter that was written on yellow legal paper. It was the only paper Dad used. I recognized his handwriting right away. He wrote with a mixture of capital and lowercase letters but mostly capital letters and he used a black fine tip pen.

The letter started out with *Dear Carolyn*, which was generic enough, but quickly turned into a letter of judgment and anger. I paced the backyard as I read how disloyal he thought I was and how he had trusted me but I ruined it. He wrote that I hurt Cindy with my selfishness and that he was disappointed that I couldn't look beyond myself. He said that he had gone through my room and found a letter I had written to a boy and that everything I had done to him and Cindy was orchestrated so that I could go back to Washington to be with the boy. The letter then went on to say that I wasn't the person Dad thought I was and that he didn't care how I lived the rest of my life and that I was no longer his daughter. My hands were shaking as I finished the letter. It was signed Ed instead of Dad and underlined to accentuate the point that he had disowned me.

I stared at his name for awhile then walked back over to the sliding glass doors. Mom was at the table with a concerned look on her face.

"Mom" I trembled, "he disowned me."

"What?" She had heard me but couldn't believe that he would do that.

"Look."

I showed her where he had signed his name and let her read the part about telling me I was no longer his daughter.

"Oh, honey... I am so sorry." She got up and gave me a hug. "Do you want to talk about it?"

"No. I just want a lighter."

I had my own lighter but since no one knew that I smoked I had to borrow Mom's. She gave me her lighter and I walked over to the burn barrel. I read the letter one more time then lit the bottom corner of the second page on fire. The flame moved quickly up the paper and I watched Dad's signature burn. Our relationship was officially over. It hurt that he disowned me but I would never let it show. The letter was meant to cause me pain. The only way I could beat him at his game was to pretend I didn't care.

Chapter 13

Dew

Nature's sweet Sumptuous
Liquid Life,
Renewing each Dawn
with its clean Refresh,
proving not Hope...
but Fate
of the coming Day.

Carolyn A. Ames

Spring came early with gifts of wild lilies and pussy willows. I ran my hand along a pussy willow branch to feel the soft silver-gray fuzz of a bud. Picking off a bud I pierced it with my fingernail and revealed the light green leaf representing new life, a sign that the bitter winter had passed. It had been a month since I burned Dad's letter. I didn't miss him at all. Thanks to my last memories of him, I had nothing left to miss.

Life at Mom and Leroy's house was better than it had ever been. They weren't drinking or fighting as much as they used to and they never asked questions about what had happened. I had talks with Mom late at night and would tell her bits and pieces but every time I tried to start from the beginning I would feel the weight of despair threaten to return. She would sense it and pat my hand, telling me that it was okay not to talk about it. Leroy had never really liked my father so it was an opportunity for him to rub it in but he never said a word. He didn't ask questions and he gave me the space I needed. Leroy and I had clashed a lot when I was younger and I had blamed him for all the fighting between him and my Mom but things had changed. My childish expectation of the perfect parent and perfect life was unrealistic. Adults were not perfect, not even close.

One late afternoon there was a long distance call for me. It was Christy's mother, Lucille. Concerned that something may have happened to Christy, I took the call in my Mom's room where it would be quite.

"Hello?" I answered.

"Hello, Carolyn, this is Christy's mother Lucille."

"Hi…is Christy okay?"

The only time I had ever talked to Lucille had been on overnights and then it was simple conversation that you would have with a friend's mom.

"Oh, yes, she's okay considering everything…" her voice trailed off.

Sensing this was more than just a call to chat I waited for her to speak again.

"Christy said you moved back to Washington because you knew the truth about what happened."

"Well, that's part of it." What did Christy tell her mom? I hadn't even talked with her since the big phone call and now her mom was calling me. Was Lucille calling to tell me she was sorry that her daughter messed everything up for me?

Lucille cleared her throat, "I was wondering if you would consider testifying against your father when we go to trial. We would pay for your plane ticket and you could stay with us."

My mind raced as I thought about how much I had loved my Dad and then quickly fast-forwarded to the disappointment I felt when I realized he wasn't the man I thought he was. I felt anger and resentment for what he had put me through and here was my chance to seek revenge. If I were on the stand, testifying at his trial, his own daughter…that would seal his fate. It would devastate him. It would prove that blood is not thicker than water and that truth is its own justice.

"No," I answered, "I can't." My voice trembled slightly. "He is my father and I won't testify against him."

"I'm sorry to hear that but I understand." Lucille didn't sound surprised.

"Is Christy there?" I asked.

"Yes, she is. Hold on." Lucille paused and then added, "Call if you change your mind."

I hadn't talked with Christy since I moved back to Washington.

"Hello?" Christy answered.

"Hi. How are you doing?"

"Okay," she said. "Sorry about Mom calling. I told her you would say no."

"That's okay." I didn't tell her that it was a little tempting.

"I didn't have to take the lie detector test." She sounded relieved.

"That's good."

We didn't have much more to say to each other and the awkward silence lingered.

"Well," said Christy, "I better go. This is long distance. I'll write soon."

"Okay, I'll talk to you later then." I hung up the phone.

I sat on Mom's bed for a little while and thought about my decision. It was the right one. What would seeking revenge do anyway? It would just cause more pain. All I had really wanted was an honest relationship with my Dad and revenge wouldn't get that for me. I thought back to Dad playing his guitar around the campfire with Donna and me singing Poems, Prayers and Promises. I wanted that back. I missed those days. He may have disowned me but I didn't disown him. You can't disown someone if you don't own them in the first place. He was my father and that would never change no matter how he felt about me. I didn't know what Dad was looking for in his life but I hoped he would find it.

* * * * *

For the next two years we heard very little from my father. He wrote a couple letters to Donna and continued to send child support each month to my mother. I had heard that he was taking college courses and dabbling in retail jewelry but I tried not to think of him too often and filled my life with excitement, which I was finding to be rather easy.

I turned 16 years old in May of 1983 and it was the best birthday of my life. My Mom put on a 60's themed party complete with a soda fountain bar, costumes and music to fit the era. Friends and family dressed up in poodle skirts and pony tails, white t-shirts and greased back hair. Everyone danced and sang…and I was in love. My life-long friend Tina had introduced me to a group of her friends and one in particular quickly lassoed my heart.

Scott had sparkling hazel eyes and curly brown hair that he attempted to tame by wearing a cowboy hat. He had a mischievous smile and a solid body that made my heart pound. Scott made a point to be romantic in every way possible from sitting on the banks of the river holding hands to watching the sun go down. We talked about our hopes and dreams. His father was away in the service so it was easy to leave my father out of our discussions. His mother was stern but with three boys I figured she needed to be since she was the only parent at home. My family invited Scott to go on camping trips and I went on trips with his family. We were very much in love and I was more than willing to give myself to him. I trusted him fully. By Christmas I was wearing a promise ring and I knew I would be married to the man of my dreams. Life couldn't be happier for me.

The following summer I broke up with my cheating boyfriend, thanks to the honesty of one of his many girlfriends. I didn't want to believe the signs that told me he was cheating…such as the hickey on his neck. He said it was a pinch hickey and I chose to believe him even though my gut instinct was yelling "He's a LIAR!" Even Donna knew he was lying and she told him so. I didn't want to believe my boyfriend was cheating on me because then I would have to address it and that would mean breaking up. It wasn't until one of his other girlfriends called me and told me how she was going to call him and tell him she was pregnant, that I had no choice but to face it. Within 20 minutes my boyfriend called to confess everything and it was over. My fairytale romance was over. Later I wondered if that was how Cindy had felt. Did she choose to believe Dad because the thought of being without him and the perfect life they had created was more difficult than living in denial? I was starting to believe that men were more trouble than they were worth.

My relationships went down-hill after the break up. I finally settled with a pot smoking, cough syrup drinking, and pill popping guy with a really nice Mustang. He smoked joints as much as I smoked cigarettes. I didn't care. I really liked his mom and there was always alcohol to drink. Plus, I was pretty sure he was too high most of the time to cheat on me. The only time I prayed to God was when I would awake in the middle of the night from bad dreams, and even then I would only pray after having at least three nightmares in a row. I was always surprised that it would work. God had to be mad at me for not going to church, smoking, fornicating, drinking and cussing. That was okay though because I was pretty mad at Him too.

In Mid-May of 1985 I flew back to Midwest to watch my class graduate. I wouldn't be graduating for another two weeks from Tumwater High so I took my homework with me and watched what could have been, if only things hadn't changed so drastically two years before. I stayed with Christy's family for a week. I was the new girl in town all over again and it felt strange to come back. The towns seemed much smaller and a lot dustier than I remembered. The dry heat felt good but my hair went limp as all the moisture evaporated into thin air.

No one mentioned my father and I was thankful for that. Lucille made delicious meals and I stayed with all four girls in the basement. They had remodeled their home to add a huge basement and the bathroom was enlarged so we could all do our hair at the same time. I had saved up money to buy a graduation dress in Washington and was excited to show it off. It was a silky pink, low cut dress that showed off my legs and I knew that I looked good in it. As I walked into the gymnasium on the day of graduation people stared at me and I swallowed hard to hide my nervousness. Were they staring at my dress or were they thinking about my father?

I paused as I glanced around looking for a place to sit. It was crowded. As I started to head toward the bleachers one of the P.E. teachers came toward me and offered to escort me to a chair next to him on the floor. I was grateful for the gesture and quickly followed him. He had dated a student a few years back and I wondered if he was interested in me. He was my father's age and as I thought about what it would be like to date an older man my skin crawled and I shivered. I was an outsider again but this time I didn't care. I was tired of worrying about what everyone thought and I was going to have fun. The townspeople had no idea who I was and this time I was not representing a cop's daughter, I was not going to church and I wasn't innocent.

There were only nine classmates graduating. I would have made it ten. When it was finally time to congratulate the graduates I anxiously awaited my turn in line. I shook hands with the guys and hugged the girls until I got to Greg. I looked at Greg and decided to give him a hug. I whispered in his ear my congratulations and hugged him a little longer than I should have. I had always wondered about Greg and if he had ever had feelings for me. He politely thanked me as his cheeks flushed a little. I remembered that he had a girlfriend and backed away. I was sure I had embarrassed him and was sorry. Quickly I moved on to the next in line.

The end of my stay came quickly. As I packed my suitcase I thought about my Dad. I had no idea if my father even knew I was in town. In a small way I hoped that he knew and that it bothered him. I wanted him to know that I could still walk in the town that he took from me and that I stayed with the family that had to deal with the crime he committed. I also secretly wished that he would find out and rush into town to talk to me, to apologize for disowning me and beg for my forgiveness.

As I thought about everything that had happened I could feel adrenaline starting to race through my veins. The move, the arrest, the phone call with Christy telling me all about their affair, Cindy dragging me up the stairs demanding I tell Dad what I had witnessed, the Bible verses I had to read and Cindy telling me I was going against God's Will all came crashing back into my mind like they had done many times over the last two years. I wanted to run into the prairie, lay down with the rattle snakes and scream at the top of my lungs. I didn't want to be an outsider and I didn't want to feel so alone. Just then the phone rang. It was Greg and one of his friends wanting to get together with Christy and me. I thought about it for less than a minute. Of course I would say good-bye to Greg. It was the only thing left in the world that I wanted to do.

The four of us drank wine coolers and drove along a dusty road up to a tower. It was dark and the stars were shining by the billions. Greg and I were in the back seat, his friend was driving and Christy was in the passenger side. Once the car was parked

Greg's friend and Christy got out and walked around the tower so it was just Greg and I left in the car. We both sat there awkwardly making conversation but both knowing why we were there. Was the attraction that we had had over two years ago real? Had we changed too much to move forward or would we find that the chemistry was enough to make us change our future plans so we could be together? Was Greg's relationship with his girlfriend enough to make him say no when temptation was sitting right next to him? I already knew that the relationship I had with my boyfriend wasn't strong enough and I had waited a long time to see if Greg and I could be soul mates.

Time was slipping by and finally Greg made the first move, sliding over to kiss me. I accepted his advance and neither of us stopped until we had our answer. Our relationship as friends was over and we were not soul mates. Whatever chemistry we had before was gone and we had made a mistake. As Christy and I were dropped off in front of her house, Greg and I politely said good-bye. It was bitter sweet to find out that what might have been could never be but I didn't regret finding out for sure because I would have always wondered.

Chapter 14

Rebuild

Dad called a week and a half before I graduated. He wanted to come to my graduation and asked if Donna and I would spend a day at the beach with him on the Saturday before my ceremony. The judge had given him special permission to come to Washington for my graduation. He hadn't been sentenced yet but the judge didn't find him as a flight risk. I didn't want to seem too happy about it since I still felt the sting of his letter two years before but I couldn't ignore the fact that I wanted to see my Dad again and that I wanted him to see me graduate. It was a one-time chance for a parent and even I didn't have a right to keep that from him.

Dad had to fly to Washington instead of the usual road trip because of time constraints so he rented a new blue Camaro with T-tops to take us to the beach for a day. Donna and I would have our own hotel room in Ocean Shores for the night and then we would head back home the next morning. We each packed a small bag and jumped in the hotrod. The weather was exceptionally warm and it was impossible to hold a grudge so I allowed myself to guardedly enjoy myself.

In an effort to break the ice Dad pulled over on the side of the highway and told me to drive. I had never driven a car so nice and with such power. I cautiously put it into drive and stepped on the accelerator until I was just under the speed limit.

"See the "O" next to the "D"? Dad asked.

I looked down at the shifter and noticed there was an extra gear with an "O".

"Ya, I see it."

"Well, that "O" stands for overdrive." Dad explained. "Step on the gas, see what this baby is made of and shift it into overdrive."

I looked at him as if he were joking but then quickly realized he was serious. Stepping on the gas I could feel the power and my heart began to beat hard.

"Alright Carolyn!" Donna cheered.

"Okay, now slam it into overdrive and give it some more." Dad smiled.

My eyes widened and my legs began to tingle as I shifted into overdrive. The engine roared as I watched the speedometer cruise to 100mph. My adrenaline was pegged as well and after a few minutes I slowed back down to the speed limit. I had never felt such a rush of power. I couldn't say a word but Dad knew what I was feeling and only smiled.

Once we arrived at Ocean Shores Dad picked up a loaf of uncut bread, a chunk of cheddar cheese and a four pack of blackberry wine coolers. Donna and I were surprised that Dad was drinking wine coolers but shrugged our shoulders. The day was strange already so the coolers just made things more interesting. As we walked down the beach Dad seemed intent on checking out the dunes and walked over to an area that was surrounded by dunes on three sides, sort of like a cove. He set the grocery bag down and started digging in the sand. By the time we walked over to see what was going on he placed the coolers in the hole.

"This will keep everything cool until we are ready for our lunch." Dad said.

"Oh. So we get a cooler too?" Donna asked.

"Yes, this is our special lunch: bread, cheese and wine." Dad replied.

"When's lunch?" Donna asked.

We all laughed. Once Dad placed the bread on top of the wine and cheese he buried it and placed drift wood by it to mark the spot. It was a rare windless day and the temperature was rising so we headed down the shore to comb the beach and talk about our plans for the future.

Dad told us that he was going to prison for a full year. They were sending him to the State Penitentiary in Rawlins – The Big House. We were silent. What should we say to that?

"They are going to put me in isolation for awhile." He added.

"What?" I asked.

"Why?" Donna demanded.

"Think about it. I was a cop. I put a lot of bad guys away, some went there."

I pictured Dad walking to his cell and a big burly criminal with tattoos stabbing him with a filed down spoon handle.

"I'm going to be a target." He added.

I had mixed emotions about what I was hearing. I was no longer a naïve child that accepted his every word. He could be exaggerating. But I also knew that what he said was true to some extent. He had put a lot of bad guys away. It made me mad that I pitied him for being in a situation that he created. Did he consider other men that had sex with teenage girls as criminals? Where did he draw the line? Still, I was afraid for him. It was as if a veil had been removed and I could see him differently. I was stronger now and didn't rely on him for my well-being. He wasn't my hero anymore. It was up to me if I wanted to have a relationship with him or not and that gave me strength.

"What will you do Dad?" Donna asked.

"I'll have to find some friends in there, quick. Maybe befriend a couple of guards so they will help watch out for me. I'll have to earn the respect of some of the lifers. I might have to fight to do that."

"Can they keep you in isolation?" I wondered.

"I've asked that same question. I won't know until I get there."

We had turned around and headed back for lunch. My scalp was burning from the hot sun. It was rare to have such warm weather at the beach this time of year. Dad quickened his pace and then began to run. Donna and I watched as he flailed his arms over his head as he screamed.

"HHHEEEYYYYYY!!!!!!! GET OUT OF THERE!!!!!"

Glancing ahead I could see a crow tearing apart our bread. It had found our stash and was enjoying our lunch. I began to wonder if the crow was going to fly away as Dad approached with his arms outstretched as if he were going to strangle the bird. As if to mock him, the crow waiting until Dad was within two feet and then it flew off with half the loaf, dropping the other half in the sand. Dad collapsed in the sand next to the loaf and attempted to brush off the sand but gave up when he realized it was of no use. Exasperated, he took a moment to assess his surroundings and then turned his gaze on us. We stood still waiting to see what he would do. A smile appeared as he announced that we didn't need bread anyway as long as we had the wine.

We sat on the beach and watched the tangerine sun set into the friendly Pacific Ocean before heading to our hotel. Dad was tired and asked if we minded ordering pizza to be delivered to our room. We were fine with that and promised not to roam the beach after he went to bed. As I lay in the hotel bed that night I thought about how we had ignored the obvious. Dad didn't say a word about disowning me or the night I confronted him in front of Cindy. It was all swept under the rug-history. I thought I would feel relieved about that but instead it felt like I was hiding something. It was easy on the outside to go through the motions of polite conversation. I knew how to behave as if nothing had happened. But it didn't make it go away; it festered like a splinter that has been covered by a thin layer of skin in an attempt to heal.

As we headed back home the next morning Dad had one more surprise for us.
"Do you remember Leonard and Debbie?" he asked.
"Yes." Donna and I answered in unison.
Leonard and Debbie attended our church. All the girls had a crush on Leonard. He was tall and had a sweet smile. His wife, Debbie, was a beautiful blonde. They didn't have any children but they were a young couple just starting out.
"What do you think about Debbie?" Dad asked.
"She's pretty." Donna shrugged.
"And nice." I added.
"Well, she's at the hotel." Dad revealed.
I was confused. Why would Debbie be at the hotel? Did she have family here too?
"We are at the hotel together."
It dawned on me then. My mouth noticeably dropped. It was a real shock. Leonard was a nice man and my Dad was having an affair with his wife. I had already gotten used to the idea of him cheating on Cindy but now it was with another married woman. Debbie was even younger than Cindy. She was only 9 years older than me.
"You and Debbie are together? When did that happen?" Donna asked.

Dad started talking about how they had started falling for each other when he would visit Leonard. As he told the story I spaced out and felt my stomach start to churn. He was like a teenager giddy with love.

"She wanted to see you guys but we decided this trip should be focused on me spending time with you. She wanted to tell you hi though." Dad explained.

I smiled as if his happiness was enough to make all their actions okay. It was the polite thing to do and I knew all too well what confronting his adultery would do. I wasn't afraid this time though. I was disappointed and very conscious of the fact that it was his life and not mine.

Graduation was right around the corner and before I knew it I was walking on stage to receive my diploma. I was wearing my silver honor cord and, turning to face my mom in the crowd, yanked it a couple times with pride. I knew she was crying and I knew she was proud of me. My Grandma and Grandpa from Kodiak, Alaska had come down for the ceremony and I was very honored to have them there. My whole family was there to watch my step-sister, Terry, and I graduate. I didn't see my father but knew he must be in the crowd somewhere.

Everyone met at the house afterward to congratulate us. Dad pulled up in the Camaro and waited for me to come over to him. He handed me a card and told me he was proud of me. He had attended the ceremony and made a point to let me know it by stopping by. I didn't care who was waiting for him at the hotel, he had made it to my graduation and that was all that mattered to me at the moment. Donna and I waved good-bye as Dad headed back to pick up his new concubine and then back to Wyoming to begin his sentence.

Chapter 15
Convergence

My Grandma secured a summer job for me up in Kodiak as a camp counselor and I spent a wonderful two months at my birth place. Kodiak was different from any other place on Earth. As soon as I stepped off the plane I could feel the wild sense of freedom and the familiar salty mist on my face. Gazing up at Barometer Mountain with its vibrant green coat of summer foliage, it was as if my ancestral cells were finally awakened. Consciously, I knew this was where I was born but I didn't expect every part of my body to be so aware and alive. This was the birth place of my mother and the surrounding islands were home to my grandmother and my great-grandmother. My ancestors fished the waters here; the wilderness provided berries to sustain them and the earth held their bones. My mother had instilled in us a sense of pride for our history but I hadn't realized that the pride I felt was actually connected to the land. It was love and belonging, not to a person but to where I came from.

I spent the summer organizing games, camping with children and partying with anyone that wanted to party. It didn't take long to forget about my boyfriend. Our relationship was hanging by a thread of boredom and it was obvious that it wasn't going to amount to anything. I felt that was enough to justify a summer fling so I threw caution to the wind and became as wild as my surroundings.

I fished for silver salmon off the beach and cooked the fresh meat in the coals of a bonfire. I listened to fishermen cuss at seals in the harbor and then seals mocking them by clapping their fins together in applause. I made love overlooking a cliff as waves slapped the jagged rocks below. I watched an outdoor play about how the Russians came to the island and enslaved the natives, taking their way of life and their language from them. My aunt made me carry a huge fish head in a plastic bag through town to my great-grandmother so she could make fish head soup. I had never felt so uncool in all my life. Once I saw how pleased my Grandma Kaba was I realized the importance of what I had done and I felt ashamed that I was worried about my social status.

On the nights that I drank too much vodka thoughts about my Dad would flood my mind and I would cry. Thinking back to the day he shamed me in front of Cindy I wished I had been stronger, tougher. My heart still felt broken after all the time that had passed. How would I mend my broken heart? I was still angry that my father wouldn't talk to me about the truth or at least admit that he had been wrong. Everything would be cleared up and we could start a new relationship if he would just say he was sorry that I had ended up entwined in his mess. I didn't need the details; I just needed him to be sorry.

As summer faded I said goodbye to Kodiak and headed back to Washington. My heart was heavy as I watched the island disappear under the belly of the plane. I would miss everything about that summer but I knew I couldn't stay.

* * * * *

It wasn't long once I returned to Washington that I moved down to Vancouver to live with my Dad's brother and his wife to try to find work. I was there about a week when I received a letter from Dad. The envelope had the city of Rawlins as the return address and I knew it came from prison. I had never received a letter from someone in prison and it made everything real to me. My father was in prison. The man that I worshipped as a little girl, the man that taught me to trust him and to trust God, was in prison. This was the man that had sex with my friend when she was thirteen years old. He was the one that helped to make her life spiral out of control. How many other girls had there been? I could think of several now that it had all become so clear.

As I sat at the dining table next to the sliding glass doors I opened the letter. Holding it up to the natural light coming in through the glass from the backyard I began to read and was shocked at what he had written. It didn't make sense at all and a twinge of panic crept up into my chest. I wondered if isolation had gotten the best of him. He wrote about how he could finally tell me some things but not everything and that people were watching his every move…probably reading all his letters. He explained that he had been working on a case for years with the CIA and that not even the local police knew about it. He wrote that he had to get close to certain people by working undercover and that even Cindy didn't know about it.

As I read the letter I felt sad. I didn't believe a word of it and wondered if he was losing his mind. I wasn't mad that he was lying but I wondered if I should even write back. I couldn't just pretend that I believed him. What would I say? *Sorry, Dad, to hear that the CIA forgot to tell everyone that you were helping them so you ended up in prison. Sorry, Dad, that the CIA made you have sex with young teenage girls and then let you go to jail.* It would be easy to just not respond. Dad had hurt me enough. I was strong now and could live without him in my life. I read the letter again. He was going crazy. I expected him to be able to cope with the isolation and to end up even having friends in prison. He could make men and women believe anything. His logic was hard to argue with and his ability to change his language depending on who he spoke with was like a chameleon changing its colors yet this letter had no logic, it was all fantasy.

Before I had decided whether or not to keep Dad in my life I received another letter. This time the letter made sense and there was no mention of the CIA which brought a great relief to me. He wrote as if I were his peer, the same age. It gave me a feeling of power but it was sad at the same time. My idea of how a father should be wasn't going to become a reality and I wasn't sure if I needed another friend.

September 30, 1985

Dear Carolyn;

This letter is highly personal so if you've begun reading it any where but alone-stop.

Don and Ana don't know as much as you do about what's going on in my personal life. Especially about Debbie. It's too hard for me right now to let 9 years of marriage go down the tubes. In fact it's hard for me to hurt anyone period.

Well recently all hell broke loose, Curt and Jeri are getting a divorce. I took Jeri's side because Curt left her. Just up and decided he didn't want to be married anymore and moved in with another girl. It put Jeri in shock, she never expected anything was wrong, just hit her hard. Jeri had no one to go to and she hurt really bad. She loves Curt so much. Well the family have to take Curt's side cause he's blood and Cindy has to too. I was kind of an asshole for helping Jeri through the pain (and that's all). Anyway while Cindy finishes law school (3 years) I figured that if this thing with Deb and I were real that we'd slowly fade our love to Leonard and Cindy so that they wouldn't care so much in the end.

But whatever can go wrong, will go wrong and it did. When I was sent here to prison Deb went off the deep end. She couldn't handle me being in here and her feeling alone. She wrote me some very explicit Love letters. I mean stuff that they put in Love Story books. She described her deepest emotions, her memories of time we shared and how she hurt being without me. Well Leonard intercepted an outgoing letter and read it. Now you see Leonard was also going away for 3 years in the army. He just passed his tests and we were also going to let Love fade away over the years so nobody got hurt bad. Now the shit hit the fan and Leonard just wrote me a note and put it in the letter of Debs telling me to explain it to him.

I don't know what he has said to Deb already but there's not much to explain. It's all pretty obvious. I set down and tried to write it as best I could hoping to salvage our friendship at least. I don't know if Leonard will tell Cindy or not so I don't know yet how far it will go. Maybe he'll just leave and go in the Army. Time always has a way of working things out.

I haven't written to Donna about it yet so you might tell her what's up when you can talk to her alone. Tenative plans are for us (Deb and I, you and Donna) to get together somewhere this summer when I get free. I don't know exactly when. If Leonard leaves, Debbie and Jeri are going to get a house of their own, like a four bedroom and when I get out I plan to stay with them (3s company) Cindy may come back though for the summer. The reason for four bedrooms is that if you come to stay or visit. If all hell breaks loose and Cindy finds out the whole deal than Deb and I will leave, probably to Salt Lake City or somewhere.

I layed here in my bunk tonight and wondered how I get into all these things. It's like helping people that are hurt but getting caught up in it myself, so I wrote a poem about myself and maybe by reading it, it will help you understand me a little better.

Love
Dad

The Heartsmith

I can't watch a heart break
And stand there like a man
My love runs deep for those who hurt
I must put out my hand.

Right or wrong, it's what I am
And guess I'll always be
My hearts too big and loves too strong
It's the way God molded me.

I guess I pick up pieces
And try to make them new
But the love I share with others
I don't take away from you.

All the love within me
Never seems to end
You can call it love, or
You can call it friend.

I can't help the feeling
When I see a heart that's torn
I have to pick it up again
And hold it till it's warm.

When love's kept as possessions
And never really free
One grows bored and tired
And gives up easily.

They seem to go out shopping
For another heart that's new
And most of them condemn me
For doing what I do.

When I fix a broken heart
And then I set it free
Love we share, while I care
Is love enough for me.

It was clear to me that Dad didn't think he had done anything wrong. He was just loving people; caring for them and saving them. He viewed himself as the actual victim…of love and of love lost. But he couldn't be a victim because victims don't choose who will victimize them. My father clearly chose who to love, who to have an affair with. There were no older women, no fat women, no mature women. His "heart" only loved the younger women. His love was particular. It was easier for him, I suppose, to think of it all as love. I thought back to the trip through Utah and how he had described the Mormons way of life. He was justifying his actions even back then. He believed he was The Heartsmith.

* * * * *

Thinking back on my life, memories of my father came to me in chronological flashes. I remembered being 4 years old as my Dad ran beside me on my new red bicycle and the Christmas I sat beside him with my little guitar as he played his. I thought about the time he was a fisherman in Kodiak and I rode in the boat watching all the jellyfish float by. I knew he wanted to raise us. He wanted to try and provide a perfect home...and a perfect step-mother. I recalled all the camping trips he took us on; the Bighorns, the Tetons to name my favorites. He had saved lives with his medical skills and taught me how to recognize a person that was in a diabetic coma. He helped to build a medical center in New Guinea and took pictures to show me their ways. He taught me how to look at the sun's position to figure out the time of day and how to read my surroundings to recognize directions. As I drifted through my thoughts I recognized my father's love and yearned for those days.

My thoughts eventually moved forward to events that weren't so happy. I remembered everything so clearly that my emotions responded unwillingly. Was the good enough to outweigh the bad? Could we start over? I wasn't sure if it would work but I was willing to try. I didn't need to know everything about my father. He could have his private life separate from me and date whomever he wanted. Our relationship would need to be on equal terms. I walked over to the drawer in the kitchen under the phone and grabbed a piece of notebook paper and a pen. I was ready to re-build. Without bowing my head or closing my eyes I spoke to God without saying a word.

"God, I know you are there. I'm not mad anymore. Help me forgive. I love my Dad and I want him back."

Standing at the kitchen counter I put the tip of my pen to the notebook paper, took a deep breath and began...*Dear Dad*.

Epilogue

My father was released from prison in June 1986. It wasn't until now, 23 years later, that I discovered his sentence had nothing to do with his relationship with Christy. He was convicted of statutory rape of a minor only after an investigation that involved my friend uncovered an incident with another girl from 1977. My father had been on patrol with an underage female cadet and they had consensual sex in his patrol car. He was not sent to prison for his relationship with my friend. Christy was only 10 years old at that time and it would be three more years before their relationship would begin. Dad made an appeal based on the girl's age and the laws that were in force at the time. His appeal is used in court cases to this day. Apparently, there are a lot of men with similar stories.

Once Dad was released from prison he moved in with Deb and Leonard for a few months before eventually moving to Vancouver, Washington. He and Deb lived together for several years before they married. He brokered diamonds and partnered with his brother to start up a jewelry store. Dad died on September 6, 1993 of a heart attack. He had just turned 46 years old.

Cindy separated from my father while he was still in prison and successfully obtained her law degree. She is happily remarried, lives in another state and practices law as an accomplished attorney. She has not wavered in her faith and is very active in her church. After nearly 10 years of silence, Cindy began communicating with my sister and I after my father died and I went to visit her with my family. We don't talk about the dark days.

Christy continued a relationship with my father off and on through the years. She came to Washington for my wedding reception in 1988 and spent some time with my father in a local hotel. Christy married a man that had a boy and seemed happy for awhile. When my father died Christy called me to find out if it was true. She admitted that she was strung out on drugs and it was obvious that she was devastated by his death. That was the last time I heard from Christy until November 11, 2009 when we reconnected through Facebook. I learned that she is happy and healthy, leading a great life. Her past is just that, the past.

Donna was pregnant her senior year of high school and worked full-time while living at home. I was her birthing coach and experienced the miracle of life. She had a baby boy named David and then graduated with her class less than 3 months later. She began working for the state when she was just 18 years old. Years later she married and had a beautiful girl named Jamie. She is a good mother. We are still very close to this day and I love her dearly.

Donna and Mandy recently reconnected thanks to the internet and are enjoying their friendship by email and social media.

I moved in with Dad and Deb when they settled down in Vancouver so I could attend a local community college. I needed to find a way to enhance my opportunities and accounting classes seemed to be the key. Deb asked me about some long red hairs she found on a towel in the back of my father's car and I bluntly told her that I thought it was obvious. After all, Deb had been that girl at one time. At that moment I made a mental note not to get too close to Deb. I wasn't going to get involved with any of Dad's extracurricular activities. My relationship with my father was one of mutual understanding; we stayed away from personal issues.

After only one week of college classes I met my future husband, Gary, during a weekend trip back to Tumwater. I commuted back and forth for only a couple weeks before moving back to Tumwater to be with him. We quickly fell in love and were married 10 months later on July 16, 1988. I was able to land an accounting job and started a new career. After three years of marriage I became a mother.

My sister and I took our families down to Dad's for weekend barbeques and we were able to build a new, stronger relationship with him one visit at a time. My father loved his grandsons. My son was only two years old when Dad died but I have pictures of their last moments together. I gaze at the pictures and am drawn back to that sunny day on September 5, 1993. One of the pictures shows my father reaching up into an apple tree as my son Jacob, wearing green overalls and a green and white checkered shirt, stands only as high as my father's knees. His eyes watch in anticipation. Dad is plucking the green apple from the old tree for his grandson, my son. They would have been great friends.

Made in the USA
Charleston, SC
10 January 2013